Mayhem Florida Panhandle
(Part One)

By
Richard Wood

Copyright 2022 by Richard Wood. All rights reserved

CONTENTS

Chapter 1   Page 4
The Acreman Family Massacre

Chapter 2   Page 12
The Wyman Home Invasion

Chapter 3   Page 24
Tragedy in McLellan

Chapter 4   Page 29
Pensacola Axe Murder

Chapter 5   Page 33
The Hinote/Bryers Murders

Chapter 6   Page 38
Killing of Henry Hicks Moore

Chapter 7   Page 41
The Curious Killing of Charles Sudmall

Chapter 8   Page 48
Milton Posse Captures Fugitives

Chapter 9   Page 53
The Edwards Murders at Mulat Bayou

Chapter 10   Page 68
Big Ed Morris and a Deadly Fish Fry

Chapter 11   Page 76
Killer On the Road

Chapter 12   Page 81
Burden of Guilt

Chapter 13   Page 91
The Hanging of Wayman King

Forward

One major drawback to researching vintage crime cases, is the lack of firsthand information. I listen to stories, (when I can find them), from people who may have heard something from older relatives about events, but you never really know what is just community gossip, or tales of actual knowledge. Most of my sources are contemporary newspaper accounts. The accuracy of these can rightly be suspect at times. I have done my best to keep them as factual as possible. As always, if anyone reading has additional information, please let me know at the contacts listed below.

These short essays I have chosen for this collection are sure to have caused intense excitement and concern among the local populace. Over the generations since, the stories have mostly faded from memory except among the older generation. Hopefully this collection, and the future stories I hope to publish will keep the memories alive.

I hope you enjoy this, and find it informative.

Richard Wood
judgingshadows@gmail.com

Facebook group:

Panhandle Mysteries and Mayhem
https://www.facebook.com/groups/271660740515949

> **WHOLE FAMILY KILLED**
>
> Milton, Fla., May 14.—W. G. Acreman, his wife and seven children were incinerated in their home near here last night. There are indications that they were first murdered and that the house was then set on fire to hide the crime. A thorough investigation is being made in hope of finding some clue that will lead to the arrest of the guilty parties.

Chapter One
The Acreman Family Massacre

On May 14, 1906, in the Allentown community of Santa Rosa County, Florida, William Glenn Acreman, his wife, and seven children were murdered, and their home burned down over their lifeless bodies. No one was ever punished for the crime.

On that morning, a neighbor, living about a quarter a mile away, looked toward the Acreman place, but did not see the house. He contacted other neighbors, and a group of them found the Acreman house in smoldering ruins. Upon closer investigation, they found the burned bodies of the family. One member of the group went to a nearby turpentine camp, and called the Sheriff's office in Milton.

Judge Rhoda, Sheriff David Mitchell, Dr. H.E. Eldridge, and several others, hurried to the Acreman home to find the ruins still smoking. A stiff northwest wind was blowing, and cinders were found a half of a mile away from the scene. It is believed that the house the Acreman's were murdered in was located on present day State Highway 87, where it is joined by Sonny Dozier Rd. Nothing remains today, but that site is approximately 10 miles north of downtown Milton, and that was the description in contemporary news accounts.

W. G. Acreman was the son of Zebulon Rudolph Acreman, and was most likely born in 1869 in Lowndes County, Alabama. He had eight brothers, and one sister. He was described as being a peaceful, pious, and harmless man with no enemies.

In 1902, the Acreman's were living in Mobile, Alabama near the corner of Selma, and Marine Streets. Described as being in desperate circumstances, they were helped by their church. Mr. Acreman was remembered there as a peaceful, harmless man who was very religious, and a bit eccentric. He had no known enemies, and apparently they left Mobile, and settled in Opp, Alabama for about a year, and sometime in 1903, moved to the area where they eventually died.

Acreman had been married at least three times. One marriage record has been found. He married Timathea Nippee, or Nipper, in Escambia Co., Alabama on 5 Feb 1893. He was also married to Mary Simmons of Brewton, Alabama. His last wife was Amanda Sorrells who died that night with her newborn baby. She was most likely the daughter of David W. Sorrells, who lived in the community of Pine Level, near Jay, Florida. Acreman had a daughter that survived. She was from his marriage with Mary Simmons, and was staying with an aunt in Selma, Alabama.

The Crime Scene

Acreman was working as a sharecropper, and the family was desperately poor. The house they resided in was described as a two-room "L" shaped house with two doors in front, one each opening into each room. Directly opposite were two doors going to the back porch. The house had numerous windows, and the front of the house was facing north. Acreman, and one son shared a bed in the southeast corner of the east room. His wife, and 3-day-old infant slept in a bed in the same room, directly opposite. Three boys slept together in the southeast corner of the west room, and directly opposite of them was the bed of two daughters, the oldest being around fourteen.

In the ruins of the house, Acreman was found near the sill of the door leading from his room to the back porch. A gun was found by his side. His skull was crushed, and upon examination a large blood clot was found at the base of his skull leading authorities to believe he was killed before the fire. His body, as all the others, was burned very badly. His wife and infant baby were found on the front porch, and it was believed they were killed outside. The condition of her skull indicated she was killed before the fire. The boys, and the younger of the two girls were apparently either killed in bed since their remains were found where their beds were located. The oldest girl was found just inside the door leading to the front porch.

There was a subscription in Milton, and Bagdad to raise money for a reward for information. An amount of $1500 was quickly raised, but there were no immediate developments in the case.

The list of contributors reads like a Who's Who of Milton in 1906:

H.S. Laird - $50, Prosecuting Attorney
David Mitchell - $100, County Sheriff
Balentine & Whitley - $50, Manufacturer, Naval Stores
Franklin S. Gay - $25, Turpentine Camp Operator
John T. Salter - $10, Railroad Carpenter
Charles E. Elliott - $100, farmer
E. M. Gainer - $50, possibly Ella Gainer, wife of Jim,
W. F. Harrison - $25
C. D. Bass - $5, Day Laborer, in 1900.
D. P. Johnson & Son - $25
Robert C. Fleming - $5, mill worker
R. E. Peterson - $5, fisherman
Howard Jernigan - $10, 1900 he was a census enumerator
Fisher & Hamilton - $50
Fisher & Co. - $50
G. L. Abbott - $5
Thomas W. Jones - $10, mercantile store
J. A. Allison - $5, keeper of Poor House
J. B. Ellis - $10, farmer
Howard S. Bates - $5, dry goods, (1910)
Cohen Bros. - $50, General Merchant
Milton Drug Co. - $25
Dr. C. B. McKinnon - $25
Frank E. Dey - $10, jewelry shop

M. N. Fisher, Sr. - $5, night watchman
I. M. Josephson - $5, dry good merchant
A. Moneyway - $5
D. T. Williams & Co. - $25
Lawrence Brown - $5
Dr. W. A. Mills - $10
The Milton Index - $10, Local Newspaper
H. C. Monroe - $5
W. W. Allen - $25
Lewis P. Golson - $50, Clerk
P. T. Macarthy - $10
D. B. Whitmire - $25, tax collector
Willis W. Harrison - $10, hatter
J. C. Gay - $10
Walter Rivenbark - $10, turpentine laborer
Allen & Allen - $25
E. P. Holley - $25, County Judge
E. L. Daniel - $25
R. M. Jernigan - $5
Lewis M. Rhoda - $5, Judge
Chaffin & Co. - $50
J. C. Day - $10
W. A. Waller - $10
R. C. Helms - $25
Morris Littles - $25
D. F. Johnson - $50
J. A. Bryant - $50
Charley H. Simpson - $25, farmer
Dr. H. E. Eldridge - $25
C. P. Jernigan - $10, butcher
J. E. Spencer - $10
Alexander H. Allen - $20, farmer

From Bagdad:

Stearns-Culver Lumber Co. - $100
B. Greenwood - $10
Asbery P. Hardy - $25, retail merchant
Bagdad Manufacturing Co. - $75
Steward Bros. - $25
Dr. B. H. Alles - $10
A.   Nicholson - $5
Capt. John Rourke - $5, sawmill owner, Confederate vet.
Aycock & Co. - $10
R. E. Barnes - $5

Ralph C. Beagle

In 1906, crime investigation was extremely primitive. There were no trained investigators in Milton, no idea about forensics, or crime scene preservation, so a reward fund would be raised, and private investigators would arrive with hopes to solve the case, and collect the reward. Eventually the reward fund reached around $2300 including $500 from the State. (*Almost $75,000 in 2022*). This was how big, headline making crimes were investigated in those days. Private Investigators, some real, some no more than con men seeking to bilk communities out of their reward money, would seek out these opportunities. The Acreman crime brought a man named Ralph Clifford Beagle, claiming to be an investigator. All that I can find out about him is that he was born, and raised in Saginaw, Michigan, and in the 1900 census he is staying in a hotel on Ship Street in St. Joseph, in Berrien County, on the eastern shore of Lake Michigan with his occupation listed as a traveling salesman. Beagle claimed he was a detective, and apparently did work hard to solve the case. About a year after the murder, Beagle physically took part in getting warrants, and making two arrests with help from local police.

In Gonzales, Florida, **William C. Smith**, (*I believe this was actually a man known as Kitchen Willie Smith., or William K. Smith. I found him buried in Monroeville, Alabama with his wife, Eliza Jessalena Smith who died on 14 April 1907.*) was arrested and brought to Milton. He was living in Allentown at the time of the murders, and when his wife died in 1907, he took her remains, and his six children to Monroeville, Alabama. Some articles suggested that he confessed, but if so, his confession must not have been believable.

In Samson, Alabama, located in Geneva County, and not far from Opp, detectives arrested **Joe Stanley**. Stanley must have had a fearsome reputation, because the detectives employed some subterfuge to get the drop on him. They visited his farm asking if he had any tacks they could use to put up a sign with. When Stanley turned to get some one of the detectives got the drop on him, and he was arrested at gunpoint. After the warrant was read to him, Stanley asked if he could get some clothes from a trunk. The detectives refused, but opened the trunk themselves, and found no clothes, but did find two pistols there. Stanley also attempted to get his hands on a shotgun, with no success. Stanley had a wife and two children, and refused to waive extradition to Florida. After the right paperwork was obtained, he was removed to Santa Rosa County, Florida.

There was a hearing scheduled for May 15, 1907 in Judge Rhoda's courtroom, and it was postponed when state witnesses could not be located, and a stenographer was not available. I found another article that claimed the prosecutor, and judge were under death threats, and did not show up for court. Regardless, two days later there was a brief hearing, and both suspects were released. The case is officially unsolved.

When Stanley was arrested, the Troy (Ala) Messenger published an article that mostly reported the same information as the other papers, but they added that, "Stanley has been under suspicion as he is said to have had trouble with the murdered man." No other references to this "trouble" could be found. When the Acreman's moved from Mobile to Opp, did Mr. Acreman have some kind of run-in with Stanley? The farm Acreman was working when the murders occurred may have been owned by the Stanley family of the Opp area.

There are many articles in southern Alabama newspapers about confrontations with the law by Joe Stanley. It's not possible to know if there were multiple Joe Stanley's living in the area during the same time frame. There was an article added to Joe Stanley's Find A Grave memorial that told the story of Jocephus Stanley's death on March 8, 1928. I pretty sure this is the same Joe Stanley that had been arrested in the Acreman murders. Stanley was a policeman in Phenix City, Alabama, which is just across the Chattahoochee River from Columbus, Georgia. In the middle of the river on an island that is sometimes claimed by both Alabama, and Georgia, Stanley was shot during a confrontation with a gang of gamblers, and bootleggers that based themselves in the "no man's land". Stanley was attempting to arrest George Chambers who was a customer of James Jennette. Stanley had been informed of some threats directed at him and went to ask Jennette about it. During the confrontation, Jennette pulled a pistol and fired three shots. Two missed, but the third hit Stanley in the stomach. Another officer hit Jennette in the head, and at the same time Stanley backed off a few feet, and fired one time, hitting Jennette in the body. They were loaded in the same car and taken to the hospital, where both died. His body was brought back to Opp where he was buried.

William K. Smith, or Kitchen Willie Smith, died in 1916, and is buried with his wife in Monroeville, Alabama.

The Acreman family is interred in one mass grave in the Jay Cemetery. The grave is next to Amanda's parents, and an older brother. Their headstone has the quote:

"No pain, no grief, not anxious fear can reach our loved ones sleeping here."

Afterword

There is a very well written book by Bill James, and his daughter, Rachel, titled: **The Man from The Train, The Solving of a Century-Old Serial Killer Mystery.**

It is the story of a long series of Axe murders across the country that occurred from 1898 through 1912. The Acreman murders near Allentown, fit right into this narrative and is covered in the book. Even setting the fire after the killing was part of the killer's technique. He quite possibly killed over 100 people in this manner and rarely left any survivors.

The Villisca Iowa killing of the Moore family is also part of this story. He makes a rather compelling case, due to the similarities among these many, many murders. The fires, proximity to railroad tracks, covering the face of some of the victims, and many more examples.

It is a very compelling case study. Were the Acreman's killed in a random manner by a psychopath riding the rails? It is hard for me to believe that Stanley, and Smith could have done something like this. I don't think it would have been the only case of this type in the area, if that was the case. Likely, we will never know for sure.

Chapter Two

The 1915 Wyman Murders

Sometime between 1905 and 1910, Guy Herbert Wyman, and his father Peter Wyman surveyed the Florida coast between Pensacola, and Destin. They purchased around 200 acres in what was then called Harris, but now known as Navarre. Guy's parents, Peter and Emily Wyman built a home on what is called Lower Pritchard Point on Santa Rosa Sound.

On June 17th 1915, neighbors of the Wyman's were getting concerned because no one had seen them, and the chickens had not been let out of the henhouse. It was noticed that freight on their dock had not been attended to. Upon further investigation, the horrific murders of the elderly couple were discovered and the authorities notified.

The Wyman's were found in different rooms. Mr. Wyman was shot, it appeared, while he was lying down, or possibly starting to rise. He had been shot once with the wounds located in his neck and left arm and shoulder. Emily Wyman had been shot at least twice, and it looked like she had been trying to flee the attackers. One was almost a contact wound as her gown had scorch marks. Deputy S.H. Lowery later testified that the head wound was the size of the palm of his hand, and there was blood and brain matter on the wall. W. W. Day, a Forest Ranger living in the East Bay area, was also one of the first on the scene and he described finding shotgun shells by a window, one on the front porch, and one on the mantle inside the house.

Santa Rosa County Sheriff J. H. Harvell arrived later on the 17th. He stopped in Holley to get the services of a physician, and undertaker. Deputy Lowery found four sets of bare footprints by the front gate and traces near a window. There was one large set of footprints and three smaller sets. The large set was peculiar and quite distinctive because the big toe was extended more than normal.

Sheriff Harvell spent a lot of time over the next couple of days examining the crime scene, and talking to people in the area. By the 19th he had four local men in custody in the Santa Rosa County jail in Milton. The four in custody were Brothers, Jim Roberts, 17 years old; Preston, (Percy) Roberts, 18, and their half-brother, William Brady Roberts, 24. Also in custody was Elder Mitchell, 19 years old. Another suspect named John Barbaree, 33, would soon be arrested also. A preliminary hearing was scheduled for June 24th. All those arrested lived in the Holley, East Bay area.

The 1910 census shows the Roberts family living in the Holley, East Bay area. Their father was John (Jake) Roberts and their mother was Dora. Brady Roberts was Dora's son by her first husband. His last name was Cordill, or Cordell, but at this time he was using Roberts for a surname. Brady was the only one of the brothers to be married. His wife was Alice (Rigdon) Roberts.

Elder Mitchell was the son of Henry, and Emmaline Mitchell who lived in the Holley, East Bay area. In the 1910 census, he was living with his widowed father near John Barbaree, and his wife, Missouri.

The motive for the killings seemed to be robbery. The Wyman's were well-off, and rumors indicated they had a large stash of money. Stolen items were two watches, two pistols, and other articles not listed. Also, in one article there is a claim that $80 was stolen. The bodies of the Wyman's were removed to the undertaker parlor on West Romana St, in Pensacola operated by Frank R. Pou. Later their bodies were shipped to Ottawa, Illinois and interred in the Summer View Cemetery. A telegram had been sent to Lt. Wyman in the Philippines informing him of his parents' deaths. Word was received that Wyman was on his way back to the states. He was going to Peoria, Illinois first, then making his way to Florida.

The Trial of the Roberts Brothers

The trial for the three Roberts brothers was severed from the prosecution of Mitchell, and Barbaree. Mitchell was talking to the prosecution at this time, and that is the most likely reason. The trial was also only for the murder of Emily Wyman. This was a hedge against the possibility of acquittal. The Peter Wyman murder trial was held back to prevent a possible double jeopardy situation.

A brief timeline: The Murders were committed 15 June 1915, and the arrests occurred on the 19th of June after a quick on-scene inquest, where evidence was examined, and witnesses called. Council was obtained on the 21st by two uncles of the Roberts boys. William Pinson Roberts, and his brother James Wilson Roberts were both doctors living in Alabama. They retained Attorney John McDuffie of Monroeville, Alabama to assist William W. Clark of Milton for the defense. John McDuffie later became a U.S. Congressman, and a Federal Judge. Observing the prosecution was Thomas F. West, the Attorney-General. He was later a Justice on the Florida Supreme Court, and a circuit Judge.

Judge: Angus G. Campbell

State Solicitor: John P. Stokes

Atty General: Thomas F. West, (conferred with Stokes, and took notes, but did not participate)

Defense: Mr. William W. Clark, from Milton, Florida.

Mr. John McDuffie, from Monroeville, Alabama.

The State had 21 witnesses listed.
Assembling the jury took about three hours.

Jury: J.H. Plant, George L. Abbott, (later named Jury Foreman), J.W. Wheeler, J.A. Nichols, J.B. Wiggins, A.B. Lewis, R.G. Payne, A.L. McArthur, E.D. Cooper, E.H. Pitts, W.E. Stanley, and I.D. Mock.

Defense asked for a continuance- denied by Judge Campbell.

Defense asked for a change of venue to Walton Co.- Judge Campbell denied.

The morning testimony were witnesses about the scene of the crime, including,

Dr. Phillips from Pensacola was called as the first witness by the state. He was the physician called to scene of murders. Testified as to the condition of bodies. Mrs. Wyman found on a bed; shotgun wound to right side of head the size of the palm of his hand. Her gown had been scorched.

Peter Wyman was found in a different room. Both had been dead 48-60 hours and decomposition had set in. He also testified that there was a hole torn in the screen where Mr. Wyman was found. He had no powder marks on his body.

Charles Cottrell: Pensacola photographer, with studios at 204 ½, S. Palafox. Took photos of the crime scene about 2-3 weeks before trial.

T. H. Lempke: Bagdad Draftsman, created a diagram of the Wyman home 2 weeks before the trial. Measurements were accurate, and the diagram was displayed to the jury and witnesses during testimony.

W.W. Day: Testified that he was a forest ranger and lived on the East Bay. He was one of the first to visit the house after the bodies were discovered. He found empty shells under a window, on the front porch, and one on the mantel. He notified Sheriff Harvell.

Elder Mitchell: Testimony: He is about 20 years old, but doesn't know for sure. He knew where the Wyman home was located. He knew the Roberts brothers, and was afraid of them. Before the killing, he talked to Barbaree, and Brady Roberts, who asked him if Barbaree ever said anything about, "going up there and take what the old folks had." Mitchell claimed he refused to go and Barbaree, and Brady Roberts said they would kill him unless he went. He said he tried not to go, and again was told he would be killed.

On the afternoon of the murders, he claimed Jim Roberts came to him and they had a talk about going up to the Wyman's house and "taking what they had". Roberts told him they were going and he would have to go. Roberts left, but later returned. Mitchell took his father's gun and Roberts had his own gun. They went over to the Sound and walked up the beach where they joined Barbaree, and Percy Roberts. At some point Brady Roberts joined them, and they all walked up the beach to the wharf near the Wyman's house. Jim, Percy, and John Barbaree went to the house. Mitchell, and Brady Roberts stayed at the wharf. The house was 150-200 yards away. Percy, and Jim were carrying the guns.

While on the wharf they heard three shots fired about an hour after the three had left and walked toward the house. Brady Roberts then left the wharf and walked toward the house, leaving Mitchell on the wharf by himself.

Shortly thereafter, the Roberts brothers, and Barbaree returned to the wharf, and Barbaree, Jim and Percy Roberts each gave Mitchell one dollar. Then they all got into the Wyman's skiff and went to the Roberts boat. They then set the Wyman skiff adrift. All were barefooted except Barbaree. They went to Oglesby's Rosin wharf about a mile away. At that time, Jim Roberts, Mitchell, and Barbaree went to Mitchell's house and stayed the night. The others stayed the night at the old mill office. (Mitchell stated that the shots he heard happened around midnight.)

Mitchell said the arrests occurred the day after the inquest. He said the killing was a Tuesday in June.

Defense Attorney Clark cross-examined him at length and succeeded in confusing Mitchell about his statements leading up to the trial. He acknowledged his fear of the Roberts brothers, and when asked why he didn't inform the Sheriff he said he was "skeered to do it". He also said he had been promised nothing for his testimony.

Ethel Mitchell: (wife) testified that Jim Roberts, John Barbaree and his wife had visited her home the day of the murders. She testified about her husband leaving with a gun that night, and returning the next morning. While testifying, she had a child in her lap that cried and wriggled, possibly shortening her time on the stand.

Mrs. Missouri Barbaree: Said on night of killing she stayed at the Mitchell house. She saw Jim Roberts with Mitchell that night.

John (Jake) Roberts: Father of the Roberts brothers. Said he could not be sure if a shotgun shown to him belonged to his son Jim. The defendant said out loud, "That's mine alright". He said Jim, and Mitchell worked for him in the turpentine business, and Percy and Brady fished for him.

Gus Harvell: Lived at the head of East Bay. He fished the Oglesby wharf, and was there with his brother Dock Harvell the night of the murders. He heard shots coming from the east. Two quick shots, and one about a minute later. Dock was asleep, but said Gus woke him up in time to hear the last shot. They were related to Sheriff Harvell.

Robert Oglesby: He knew the Wyman's and had worked for them. He was the person who found their bodies.

S. H. Lowery: Deputy Sheriff. Found tracks around the house of barefoot men. He told of seeing footprints near the front gate, and slight traces near a window. The prints were from multiple bare-footed men and one set of prints of shoes. One set of footprints were larger than the others. It was peculiar due to the abnormal extension of the big toe. During the inquest, Brady Roberts foot was compared to the peculiar set of prints, and found to be a perfect fit. He also testified that he found trunks open and contents disordered. Several empty pocket books were found.

Next day's testimony:

Sheriff Harvell: Called to the Wyman house at Lower Pritchard Point on Santa Rosa Sound on June 17. He stopped at Holley to get a Physician, and an undertaker. He then testified about methods used to compare exploded cartridges found at Wyman house with cartridges exploded for the jury. The finding was that the guns taken from the defendant's homes were the murder weapons.

The Jim Roberts Letters:

Jim Roberts, while in jail, wrote a series of notes intended for Elder Mitchell. Roberts was imploring Mitchell not to testify against the brothers, and repeatedly confessed to the murders.

The notes were given to a prisoner named G.W. White while the brothers were in the Escambia County jail. Instead of passing them to Mitchell, White gave them to the authorities.

Chief Deputy C. J. Hoffman of Pensacola testified to a conversation he overheard between Roberts and White in which Roberts told how he shot the Wyman's.

Jim's notes:

G. W. White testified about the notes. He was in the county jail in Pensacola.

1st note: *"Elder, don't tell nothing on me, for I like you, and if you was to tell all you know on me and Purce and John it would go hard on us. You know you did not go to the house, you ought to went. Don't forget me Elder. I am sending this by G.W. White. From your old friend, Jim Roberts."*

2nd note: *"Hello Elder, How are you getting along. I am worried bad, Elder. I don't believe you will tell anything on me and Percy and John and Brady. If you won't tell that I won't ever forget you Elder. You know you wouldn't go to the house. That is the reason I wrote this. Don't tell this for God's sake, Elder. I don't think you will Elder. John said when we was at the house, he said 'that boy is a-going to tell this Jim. We ought to have made him come along.' Well I guess I will stop for they might catch me writing and then I would be up against it. I am sending this by White. He is all right, I think. Don't forget me old boy. From Jim Roberts"*

3rd note: *"Well Elder, this is the last one that I am a-going to write you, and now Elder if you tell this, we'll put it all on you, for there is four against one and you know that. Elder I don't believe you will tell what you ---- on us. John said you would tell it. I told him you wouldn't Elder. Me and Purse done all the work, so don't tell it on us, for God's sake. Well I won't write no more, so good-bye, my old friend. Jim Roberts"*

When the jury was presented with the notes, it was absolutely quiet in the crowded courtroom. Every jury member scrutinized the notes carefully.

White said Roberts told him how he had shot the old man when he started to arise, and he fell after being shot, with his feet hanging over the side of the bed. White was in jail for selling liquor without a license. He had resided in Century for about a year.

After learning Mitchell had given the letters to the authorities, and seeing him at the courthouse, Roberts told him he would have people in the courtroom who would get him when he got out.

Alibis:

Percy, (19) said on the night of the murder, he and Brady were on Santa Rosa Sound fishing, and had been there for two weeks. They had a net and two skiffs. He claimed Brady was wearing shoes. Brady also claimed he was fishing at the time of the murders.

All three Roberts were found guilty with no recommendation for mercy for the killing of Emily Wyman. The jury deliberated for 30 minutes.

Elder Mitchell gave self-serving statements implicating the others in the murder. If Jim Roberts had not written the notes, and kept his mouth shut, there would have only been circumstantial evidence against them. Chances are they would have been convicted anyway, but Mitchell's testimony, along with the letters, sealed their fate.

In August, all three were sentenced to death by hanging which would have happened in Milton.

Later, eight jurors wrote to the state parole board asking for mercy. In December 1916, the parole board commuted the sentences to life.

There was a trial in November 1915 was for the murder of Peter Wyman in which the Roberts brothers, and John Barbaree were found guilty of his murder, and all sentenced to Life in prison. This trial had the same witnesses and testimony of the first trial except that Lt. Guy Wyman, son of the murdered couple, testified that a watch recovered from the Roberts home had belonged to his father.

Elder Mitchell, (probably in the Hall of Fame for jailhouse snitches), pleaded guilty to two counts of 2nd degree murder, January 1917, and was given a life sentence.

In the Pensacola News Journal on 28 June 1917, it was reported that all five convicted for the Wyman murders were loaded on a train, and sent on their way to Raiford, the Florida State Prison.

Elder Mitchell's Prison Break

From the Tampa Tribune, 14 June 1923:

Elder Mitchell, and a convicted murderer from Panama City, named Leslie Layman, escaped from the Captain Willis Road Camp near Ehren, Fla, which is east of New Port Richey in a swampy area. They escaped on 10 June, and were recaptured on Wednesday afternoon, June 13.

At 2 pm on the 13th, Deputy Sheriff L.B. Lennon received a call from the Chapman district, where two men had attempted to steal a "large touring car" from a private garage.

Accompanied by Constable James Stokes, he found Layman being held by three men. Layman admitted his identity, and was taken to the county jail. Lennon contacted Captain Willis, and along with Stokes, began searching for Mitchell. Soon Willis arrived with bloodhounds, and a small posse. The hounds tracked Mitchell to a secluded neighborhood east of Chapman where an old friend of Mitchell lived. He was taken into custody there.

Mitchell had been a trustee at the Camp for seven years.

Layman had been convicted of killing a woman in Panama City in 1920. He killed her, stole her car, and drove it to Alabama, where he was captured.

Parole

It seems that once upon a time, if you got the death penalty, you would usually be executed within a couple of years. Apparently, life sentences meant that you would serve around ten years, (at least in this case). There was an article in the Tampa Tribune on Sept. 7, 1924, "Pardon Board will Decide on 81 Pleas." The three Roberts brothers were listed. Jim Roberts was pardoned April 1, 1925. His brothers were pardoned around the same time, but I could not find a newspaper report. Mitchell, and Barbaree were pardoned in 1929.

Jim Roberts Lawsuit

In May of 1929, there was a report of a lawsuit, and subsequently a bill introduced by the state legislature to compensate Jim Roberts, who was living in Bagdad, Florida since his parole. On Dec. 15, 1922, the Raiford prison doctor J.L. Chalk operated on Jim for appendicitis.

Apparently, he left forceps inside Roberts' abdomen which caused constant pain until removed in another operation on March 13, 1929. The compensation was $5000.

Epilogue

In March of 1929, the Tampa Times reported that Elder Mitchell was pardoned. The same article stated that citizenship had been restored to John Barbaree. I'm not sure if it is the same Barbaree, but it probably is.

In Feb. 1935 Elder Mitchell and his wife were seriously injured while passengers in a truck driven by Ossie Rigby, who died in the crash. Five miles south of Crestview, they ran into a parked car on the side of the road with no lights. They were taken to the Enzor Hospital. The Mitchell's were living in Ft. Walton Beach at the time. Elder Mitchell died on 28 August 1946.

John Preston (Jake) Roberts, father of the Roberts brothers, in 1920 was running a boarding house in Bagdad with his wife, Dora, on River Front Water Street. In 1924, Dora died in Bagdad, and is buried in the Bagdad cemetery. In 1930, Jake is either remarried, or cohabitating with a woman named Emma. I could not find a marriage record. By 1935, maybe using Jim's settlement money, they had relocated to East Tampa, in Hillsborough County. In 1940 he was living in the same place with Jim and was listed as a widower. He died in 1948 and was buried in the Providence Cemetery in Hillsborough County.

By 1930, Brady was living in Deland, Florida; 1940 in Volusia County, Florida; 1945 in Duval County. At some point he began using the Cordell surname, and died in Duval County, July 19, 1964.

John Preston "Percy" Roberts died in Hillsborough County, Florida on March 9, 1977.

James Milton "Jim" Roberts died in Hillsborough County, Florida on June 1, 1970.

John Barbaree was paroled in 1929. In September of 1933 he took up residence in Pahokee, Florida, which is located on the southeast side of Lake Okeechobee. He was working for the Southern Sugar Company, and in March of 1934 allowed a man named J.C. Morton to move in with him. On April first, the body of John Barbaree was found 3 miles east of Indiantown, Florida. Supposedly Barbaree had $200-$500 on him from the sale of some property. His money, his car, and his roommate were missing. Through investigation it was determined that Barbaree was most likely attacked while he was asleep. He had a wound near his temple, possibly from an ice pick, and he had been hit in the head with a blunt instrument. It is thought he was killed around 10 pm on Saturday night, wrapped in a tarpaulin, and dumped where his body was found. Nothing more on J.C. Morton could be found.

Lt. Guy Herbert Wyman.

Wyman had an interesting life. There is much written about him and his life in the Panhandle. He sold much of the land he owned on Santa Rosa Sound to developers, and his war-bride Noelle gave it the name, Navarre.

Later Wyman and Noelle were divorced, and he remarried. The Pensacola News Journal on July 15, 1932 reported that Wyman had shot and killed his ex-wife Noelle when she showed up at his home. This was the same house that his parents died in back in 1915. He shot her twice with a 30-30 rifle when she threatened his new wife. He claimed self-defense, and was acquitted in trial. During the depression Wyman sold some of his land to the county, and part of that parcel is now Navarre Park.

Chapter Three

The McLellan Tragedy

It was Sunday morning, June 24, 1934.

Luther D. Padgett, known as L.D., and his wife Daisy were making the three-mile walk from their once shared home to the residence of her parents. L.D. was walking slightly behind Daisy, and simmering with sadness and anger that she had refused his efforts to reconcile and move back in with him. They had been separated since Christmas. He later told Sheriff Joe Allen, "I loved her and I couldn't stand to see her go." Using a turpentine hack, he hit and slashed her in the back, and as she fell, struck her in the neck, chest, and stomach. As he dragged her off the road and into the woods, she begged him to let her see their two small children once more before she died. He left her moaning and dying in the woods. He disposed of a bundle she had been carrying in a nearby creek, and tossed the murder weapon into some bushes.

Padgett returned home and tried to sleep, but it was too warm. He walked to a nearby friend's house, then actually visited some of Daisy's family, before returning home to be met by Sheriff Joe Allen and placed under arrest. Padgett almost immediately gave Allen a confession.

Sheriff Allen had been notified earlier of the discovery of a body by a cattleman named Ed Fuqua. Mr. Fuqua had been walking down the road looking for some of his cattle and noticed blood on the side of the road and drag marks going into the woods. He found Daisy's body and, leaving his young son at the scene, he went to find a telephone and reported it to the Sheriff.

The events described occurred very near the Alabama, Florida state line near McLellan. Daisy was the daughter of Lawrence Clayton Locklin, and Hattie Mae Fleming Locklin. Her younger brother was Lawrence Hankins Locklin, also known as Hank Locklin, the very popular country music artist. She was employed at a restaurant in

Brewton, Alabama. She and L.D. Padgett were married in Escambia County, Alabama on March 30, 1929. At the time of her death, they had a four-year-old son and a baby daughter who were subsequently raised by her parents. Daisy was buried at the McLellan cemetery.

L.D. Padgett was the son of Robert Lee Padgett, and Mary Blanche Smith Padgett. Many of the family members from both the Padgetts, and the Locklins are buried at the McLellan cemetery.

Justice Timeline

26 Sep 1934. L.D. Padgett was indicted by the grand jury on a charge of first-degree murder. The court appointed attorney's J.T. Wiggins, and T. Franklin West of Milton to represent Padgett. The prosecutor was E. Dixie Beggs, and Judge L.L. Fabisinski would hear the case.

29 Sep 1934. L.D. was convicted of first-degree murder without recommendation of mercy by the circuit court jury and sentenced to death in the electric chair at the state prison in Raiford by Judge L.L. Fabisinski. The trial lasted most of one day and the jury deliberated for 30 minutes before returning the verdict. Padgett had made an oral confession to Sheriff Allen, and later a full written confession after his arrest.

8 Oct 1934. Padgett was transferred to the county jail in Pensacola to await transfer to Raiford. Sheriff Allen stated that he had received orders from Governor Dave Sholtz to bring the prisoner to the Escambia County jail. He said he did not know the reason for the transfer.

27 Sep 1935. Padgett appealed his death sentence on the grounds that the crime was not premeditated, but the Florida Supreme court reaffirmed his death sentence.

2 July 1936. A hearing was scheduled to ask the State Pardon Board to commute his sentence to life. Also scheduled was a hearing for a convicted wife murderer from Pensacola named Lee Clark. T. Franklin West was there to represent Padgett. Judge Fabisinski, who sentenced Padgett to death, said he did not believe the crime was cold-blooded in nature, and that a commutation should be granted. The hearing was then delayed.

5 Aug 1936. The State Parole Board denied the application to commute the Padgett, and Clark sentences to life, and Governor Sholtz signed the death warrants for both men. The date of execution was set for the week of August 17. State law required a condemned man to serve five days in the death house at the state prison before the execution. The prison superintendent fixes the day and time for all executions.

17 Aug 1936. The date of the scheduled execution. Padgett was to be put to death at 11 a.m. with Clark following shortly after. Sheriff Allen from Santa Rosa County, and Sheriff Gandy of Escambia County made the trip to Raiford. State law, at the time, required the Sheriff of the county in which the crime was committed, to pull the switch himself, or appoint a deputy. Sheriff Allen had executed a convicted murderer named Ed Bradley a few weeks before.

The two condemned men had their last meals, had talked to their spiritual advisors, and had their heads shaved. Thirteen minutes before Padgett was to be put to death, Governor Sholtz called from Roanoke, Virginia, to grant Padgett a 30 day stay of execution. He wanted to have another clemency hearing before the State Parole board. A delegation of citizens from Milton wanted to appear before the board. The prison superintendent on his own authority delayed Clark's execution also to give his attorney R. L. Reece of Pensacola, time to seek a stay of execution for him. Since Clark was a black man, I wonder if the authorities did not want it to seem as if Padgett was getting favorable treatment.

14 Sep 1936. "Please spare the life of my son," was the plea from Padgett's mother. His application for clemency was supported by a group of citizens from Milton, but there were also letters of protest from the prosecuting officials and other citizens. Clemency was once again denied by the board.

Execution Day

19 Oct 1936.
4 MEN DIE IN RAIFORD CHAIR WITHIN HOUR
State Carries Out First Quadruple Execution.

This was the headline in the Tampa Tribune on 20 Oct 1936.

The first two were executed for the slaying of a Miami druggist during a holdup in 1932.

Next was L.D. Padgett. From the article: "With a bewildered look, Padgett entered the chamber, paused for a moment, then took his seat in the chair. Head bowed to watch the guards adjust the straps, Padgett began to mumble a prayer, words of which could not be distinguished by the witnesses. He still was praying at 11:05 a.m. as Sheriff Allen threw the switch. He was pronounced dead seven minutes later."

Clark took his turn in the chair and died at 11:18 a.m.

Both Lee Clark, and Luther D. Padgett were buried in the Prison cemetery.

Pensacola, Florida,
July 3d, 1934.

I, L. D. Padgett, having been told by the State Attorney that I do not have to make any statement unless I want to, and that anything that I might say might be used against me, make the following voluntary statement about the killing of my wife, Daisy Lee Padgett; I have not been promised any reward or told that the making of this statement will help me in any way, but make the same freely and voluntarily:

My wife and I had been having a lot of trouble, she was staying with her Mother and keeping our two children there and would not come to live with me. She left me just before Christmas. On Saturday night, June 23d, she spent the night at my place but would have nothing nothing to do with me. She would not even let me kiss her. About daylight Sunday morning we started over to a girl's house and then I guess we were going from there to her Mother's. As we left she told me to bring the turpentine cutter along. I think she wanted it to sharpen some knives of her Mother's. I put it in my pocket rolled up in a piece of paper. As we walked along the road we talked about the way she had been acting and one word led to another. I was pretty mad about it all and finally pulled the cutter out of my pocket and stabbed her in the back. I was walking along behind her then and she did not see what I was doing. We had walked about a mile from home. She fell down after I stabbed her in the back and then I cut her several times on the neck and once or twice in the stomach while she was lying down. She said "O, don't do that" when I was cutting her. She then told me to meet her in heaven and said she wished she could have seen the children before she went. After that I drug her off the road a piece and she did not talk anymore but she kept grunting and making all kinds of noises and pawing with her hands. When I left there she was still grunting.

I picked up the things that were scattered around on the ground and carried them about a half mile away and threw them in a branch. This included some dresses, shoes, cloth, a bag and first one thing or another that she had bought in town on the day before. I thought the cutter off in the bushes near the branch. I went on back to the house and from there to my Mother's. I lay down across the bed and tried to sleep but it was too warm. From there I went by my wife's mother's house but almost most of the folks were not there. I saw a brother of my wife and my two children and my brother's children. I did not go back by the place where I killed her.

I did what I did before I thought and realized what I was doing, and what caused me to do that was the way she was treating me after several times promising to do better.

L P Padgett

STATE OF FLORIDA
ESCAMBIA COUNTY:

Before the undersigned authority this day personally came L. D. Padgett who being duly sworn on oath says that the foregoing statment made by him is true, and that he made the same freely and voluntarily, without any force, coercion or promise of reward.

Sworn to and subscribed before me
this 3d day of July, 1934.

L P Padgett

Chapter Four

Pensacola Unsolved Axe Murder

What is now a segment of W. Hilary St. in Pensacola, once was known as Chipley Alley. It lies just south of W. Garden St. between S. Coyle St., and S. Reus St. It was near the site of the old Frisco railroad freight and passenger terminal building. On the night of July 4, and early morning of July 5, 1926, 410 Chipley Alley was the site of a vicious attack on two adults, and two children by an ax-wielding madman.

Preston Pickerin, a 23-year-old carpenter, and his wife Hattie had spent part of the evening of July 4th in Cantonment at an Independence Day celebration, where Hattie won a cake. Two children, 6-year-old Emmett Simpson, son of Hattie from her previous marriage, and 13-year-old Lucille Cushings, Hattie's little sister, had remained home.

A neighbor, Mrs. Ella Martin was awakened just before dawn, by a low rumbling sound she could not identify, and got up to investigate. She walked outside, and looking through the Pickerin's window. Seeing the gruesome scene, she ran inside screaming, "Hattie, Hattie!" She later said that Mrs. Pickerin had mumbled something and lapsed into unconsciousness. In the adjoining room lay the two battered children, still clinging to life.

Mrs. Martin called the police, and requested they bring an ambulance. The first officer on the scene was Captain J. R. Simmons, followed soon by Chief of Police William O'Connell. The officers found the room in disarray, and the walls covered in blood. There was evidence of a struggle in the adult's room.

An ax covered with hair, and blood was found in the children's bed. The ax was delivered to fingerprint expert Robert Forrest, and after extensive examination, he could find no usable prints. A shoe was also found in the house that showed a defect in the sole that matched shoe prints found outside in the unpaved alley.

As the rumors spread through the local community, a crowd began to gather to view the scene of the crime. All four victims were transferred to the hospital. Mr. Pickerin was near death and was only given a few hours to live. His wife Hattie was unconscious with severe gashes to her head. At this time, the children were reported near death, but a few hours later they regained consciousness. They both could not remember what happened. They had been attacked while asleep, and had no memory of the assault.

    The police canvassed the neighborhood, questioning neighbors, friends, and acquaintances. They discovered that bad blood existed between Pickerin and a man named Taylor. As recent as June 28th, members of Pickerin's family had appeared as witnesses against Taylor. Taylor and other members of his family were brought in for questioning. (I haven't been able to find out what the problem was between the families.)

    The authorities, being concerned about a growing lynch mob atmosphere, beefed up security at the jail in case they were attacked by vigilantes. Preston J. Pickerin died from his injuries at one pm on July 5th. His wife, Hattie, was still in a coma.

    Hours after Pickerin died, Justice of the Peace Judge Dan S. Nee summoned an inquest. On Wednesday, July 7, a six-man jury met at Nee's office. Neither the police or the Jury could figure out a motive for the attack. Robbery was discounted because the Pickerin's were not wealthy, and nothing was known to be missing from the house.

    Eleven suspects were picked up and held for the investigation, but ultimately none were charged with the crime. Chief O'Connell told the press, "This case is being thoroughly investigated and we expect sensational developments any minute."

    Police talked to a man named J. H. Perkins, a train dispatcher for the St. Louis and San Francisco railroad. He told officers he had seen a man from the railroad yard the night of the murder. "I first saw him coming from the direction of the Pickerin house. He entered several yards, and searched through some wood piles. I saw him in one yard swinging an ax in his hands, then I saw him go toward the Pickerin home." He described the man as being burly with black hair.

    The Coroner's Jury heard all this testimony, including from the eleven witnesses/suspects being held, but all the evidence was considered weak, and circumstantial. With no new information coming to light, the hearing was postponed.

On Thursday, the eighth of July, the Governor of Florida, John Martin arrived in Pensacola for the grand opening of the newly constructed Pensacola Bay Bridge. An estimated 10,000 cars crossed the bridge in the first 12 hours it was open.

The next day, Hattie Pickerin came out of her coma. She remembered seeing a man. She did not know who he was. She remembered waking up when her husband was attacked, and she believed she struggled with the assailant, but with no identification, the investigators were at a loss.

Chipley Alley was now known locally as, "Ax Murder Alley". All but 3 of the eleven suspects were released.

During the investigation of the crime scene, police did find three, five-gallon kegs of homemade liquor. The Federal authorities joined the investigation to find out the origin of the illegal booze. After a brief probe, they determined that the illegal whiskey had nothing to do with the attack.

On July 28, Judge Nee resumed the inquest, calling 23 witnesses, including Captain Simmons, and Hattie Pickerin. Mrs. Pickerin took the stand and related all she could remember from the night of the attack. After she concluded without revealing any new information, a man stood and approached the witness stand. When asked if she recognized him, Hattie said no, she had never seen him before.

The man, (whose name was never revealed in court, and referred to as, "Mr. X" in the papers.), asked her, "Is it not true that you accompanied me on a party at Bayview and had a pistol which you used to shoot a spider on a tree?" Confused, Mrs. Pickerin said, "No! I never did such a trick and besides I don't know you. I have never seen you before!" After Hattie stepped down, the stranger swore under oath that she had accompanied him to Bayview and fired a pistol at a spider.

(This whole testimony is bizarre to say the least. Not only is any such occurrence irrelevant to the case, but what exactly was she being

accused of? Why was this witness not identified? I don't believe this would ever be allowed in a courtroom today.)

At the conclusion of testimony, the jury verdict predictably was that the crime was, "committed by a party, or parties' unknown."

In 1950 a man named Robert Raymond Lassiter, in Greenville, South Carolina, confessed to the murder of Mr. Pickerin. He was arrested and brought to Pensacola, but was determined to be insane and sent to the state hospital in Chattahoochee until he could be found sane enough to assist in his own defense.

In February 1959, it was determined that his mental condition had deteriorated, and there was going to be no prosecution. The only evidence against him was his own confession, and he claimed no motive other than being drunk, and only remembered attacking one person. He was released into the custody of his family, who were going to put him in a private institution.

This crime is also unsolved, and probably always will be.

Hattie got married to Aulice McKenzie in February 1928, but divorced in 1930. She lived until 1950, passing away in Pensacola.

Lucille Cushing married Lloyd Williams, and passed away in 2006. She was buried at Pensacola Memorial Park.

I could not find out what became of Emmett Simpson. There was more than one person of that name in Pensacola, but this one is hard to find.

It seems that it wasn't very hard to get away with murder in the Florida Panhandle in the early part of the 1900's. I think that unless there were credible eyewitnesses, or someone was caught red-handed, there was little chance of prosecution.

Chapter Five

The Hinote/ Bryers Murders

Arthur Hinote, born, 7 Mar 1914, and Bernice Bryars, born, 27 Sep 1916, left the house of Arthur's sister at 1000 E. Brainerd St., in Pensacola to go to a movie. When the two did not return that night, their families began to search. They even made inquiries to neighboring states to see if a marriage license had been applied for, suspecting they may have eloped.

Arthur worked at a mattress factory, and gave most of his money to his mother. On the night of their date, he only had seventy cents in his pocket.

The next day, shortly after noon, two wood cutters, John Engstrom, and John Birthright, were looking to collect some wood near Bayou Texar, about a mile north of Bayview Park. At the time, this was a secluded area with little traffic. Engstrom saw an automobile parked in the distance, and being curious, went to take a look. Horrified, he saw the body of a young man lying next to the running board with part of his face blown away. He turned to call his partner, and saw the body of a young lady lying about 15 feet away on the other side of the car.

The young man had been obviously shot in the face. The young lady had been savagely beaten to death. It was later found that she had a deep mark on her forehead, a deep looking wound behind her ear, jaw broken in three places, and one of her eyes was discolored.

Authorities were notified and began to arrive at the scene, and along with them, a growing crowd of gawkers began to gather. Police identified the couple as Arthur Hinote, and Bernice Bryars, and notified the families. Police found few clues. There were several wads from expended shotgun shells near the bodies. The ground around Arthur was pretty much undisturbed, but it looked as if Bernice had put up quite a fight. Her watch stopped at 10:15 pm, but not due to the need for winding. Some Bayou residents reported that they had thought they heard gunfire around 10 pm.

Sheriff Mose Penton, Chief O'Connell, and Inspector Andrew Schmitz traveled to Andalusia, Alabama to interview a young man who had worked with Hinote in a sausage factory months before the slaying. The young man had an alibi, and was cleared of suspicion.

On Sunday, a dual funeral was held in the home of Arthur Hinote's parents at 1118 W. Chase St. Burial was at St. John's Cemetery, attended by approximately 5000 people. The two young victims were buried side by side.

The next day Sheriff Penton announced to the press that there were no new leads. He could not find a motive. It wasn't robbery. It wasn't revenge because there were no known enemies. He declared it to be the work of a maniac.

By Monday, rewards for the apprehension of the killer reached $550. City Manager George J. Roark put up $100. The county offered $250. State Attorney Purl G. Adams in Crestview contributed $100, and a private citizen, Joseph Banman, put up $100.

County Solicitor Richard H. Merritt joined the investigation, and Florida Governor Doyle E. Carlton sent a special investigator to lend a hand. Every day, at least a dozen investigators scoured Pensacola for leads. Interviewing, double checking, back tracking, and tirelessly seeking answers, they were getting nowhere fast.

Finally, 15 days after the murders, Solicitor Merritt announced that he was holding a suspect named Grady H. Faulk, 25 years of age. Merritt said he would give evidence to the Grand jury, and seek a true bill. Even though every effort was made to keep the evidence secret, the details began to leak.

- The evidence included a bloody shirt found in Faulk's home in Klondike.
- A shotgun of caliber that killed Hinote with a bent barrel was in his possession.

- Rumor of a compact belonging to Bryars found in his home.

The evidence was purely circumstantial, but it was strong enough for the Grand Jury to return two first degree murder indictments against Faulk. The court appointed Attorney Ernest E. Mason to defend Faulk.

On the 8th of March, 1932, the trial began. The State's case, based on circumstantial evidence, was built on these points:

- Faulk left home the night of October 22nd, carrying a shotgun.
  - -He didn't return home until 3:30 in the morning, drunk.
  - -Someone noticed blood on his shirt.
  - -He became increasingly nervous, and didn't return to work the day after the murders.
  - -Vanity case similar to Bryars found in his possession.

Faulk himself took the stand and withstood vigorous examination calmly while answering all questions put to him.

The Defense's case:
    Faulk DID return to work the next day and the rest of the days of the week.
    The shotgun in question was a 20-guage, not 12-guage used in the murder.
    He was in possession of a shotgun but a witness backed up his story that he took it from an acquaintance named Nora Coleman when she attacked him with it. He bent the barrel on a table while he was trying to break it.
    The blood on his shirt was turkey blood.
    The vanity case in question was never proven to belong to Bryars.

The same night the trial concluded; the jury took 25 minutes to acquit on the first ballot. The case then went cold for over 29 years.

On May 1, 1951, Sheriff R. L. Kendrick arrested a 58-year-old man at a Crestview bus depot. The law had been looking for this man because they had been told that he had been in a car accident with Hinote several months before the murders. Allegedly, he had threatened Hinote's life when he was forced to pay repair charges stemming from the accident. Due to lack of evidence, he was released.

With no more evidence, the case has never been solved. The killer of Arthur Hinote, and Bernice Bryars has never been identified.

It was 1931, and the field of sex crimes was in its infancy. I think this was the motive that Sheriff Penton could not, or did not want to publicly acknowledge. This kind of crime became more common with the "Phantom Killer" in the 1940's in Texarkana, Arkansas, and later the Zodiac killer in the San Francisco area around 1969-1970.

I believe this young couple found a secluded spot for parking, and were accosted by someone with a shotgun who forced Arthur out of the car and shot him. Then he assaulted Miss Bryars, and afterwards beat her to death.

It is nice that their families buried them together. They had been together as a couple for months, and all indications were that they would be married.

Recent photograph of Bernice Bryars and Arthur Hinote, youthful pair, called sweethearts, whose bodies were found shortly before noon yesterday in the woods a short distance north of Bayview park. They had apparently been murdered late the night previous. Hinote had been killed by gunshot, according to a coroner's jury, while his girl companion is believed to have been beaten unconscious, assaulted and then slain.

From Pensacola Journal, 24 October 1931

Chapter Six

The Unsolved Murder of Henry Hicks Moore

There was another killing in a secluded parking area, before the Hinote, Bryars, killings. The location of this one was in the Magnolia Bluffs area off of Scenic Highway. This occurred months before the last one I wrote about, and is also unsolved.

Henry Hicks Moore left his wife and son at home on the evening of January 10, 1931 and went to the Saenger Theater to watch a movie. He was not alone. He had a date with a 19-year-old Miss Gretchen Gregory. Moore was 23 years old and lived at 503 E. Jackson St., with his wife Eulalie, and son Henry, Jr. Later, Miss Gregory claimed she had no idea that Henry was married.

After watching "The Painted Desert", they jumped in Henry's roadster and drove toward East Pensacola Heights, stopping to get a soft drink at a roadside sandwich shop, then proceeded to the area of Magnolia Bluffs on Scenic Highway. About 11 pm Moore parked his car down a secluded path about 75 yards from the main road.

Just a few minutes after stopping, two men, each shining a flashlight into the couple's eyes, shouted for them to, "Stick 'em up!". Miss Gregory screamed and one of the assailants shot Henry Moore, and then they disappeared in the woods. After sitting in shock for a moment, she climbed over Henry and got behind the wheel. She heard him mumble something, but didn't understand what he said. She had only driven a car once before, but after a few attempts was able to get the car started and back out on the highway. She first stopped at a closed drug store, but finding no one there, she drove to Pensacola Hospital. (Later Sacred Heart on 12th avenue) Her arrival time there was noted as 11:40 pm.

Ten minutes later, Dr. C. C. Webb pronounced Moore dead. The police were notified. Sheriff Mose Penton was notified since the crime occurred outside city limits. Miss Gregory gave him the details of the night's events. When Gregory was informed that Henry Moore was married with a family, she was shocked. The police went to the scene of the crime but found no evidence. The only prints they could find on the car belonged to Moore, and Gregory.

The Officers did discover, however, two $2000 life insurance policies, payable to the victim's wife. One of them had only been written that day.

Miss Gregory was held overnight in jail as a material witness, pending the outcome of the coroner's inquest and questioned repeatedly, but her story did not change. The autopsy was performed by Dr. James W. Hoffman, and showed the cause of death as a bullet through Moore's heart that passed at a downward angle and came to rest in his back by the 8th rib. The bullet was identified as a .38 caliber. Powder burns indicated he had been shot at close range. Miss Gregory was released on $7500 bond, and her family retained Attorney William Fisher to look out for her best interests.

A reporter interviewed Henry's widow who claimed Henry hardly ever went out at night. He had been home for supper, and played with his son for a little while before kissing her goodbye, and heading for the movie.

On Wednesday, a capacity crowd gathered in the courtroom of Justice of the Peace Dan A. Nee to hear evidence on the Moore case. Testimony was heard from seven witnesses including hospital and police personnel, but the star was Miss Gretchen Gregory. She repeated the detailed sequence of events of that night, and the jury found that Henry Hicks Moore died "at the hands of an unknown person, or persons."

On February 19, State Attorney Fabisinski called a grand jury to once again investigate the case trying to find new evidence. Even though the Associated Press had reported that Moore's brother-in-law, R. S. Clark of Greenville, SC, claimed to have furnished clues to Pensacola police officers; the grand jury found no new information about the case.

The murder of Henry Hicks Moore remains unsolved to this day.

Gretchen Gregory married Henry C. Longuet on June 30, 1931 in Santa Rosa, County. In the 1940 census they were living on 81st Street in New York City, with a three-year-old daughter, and her husband was a Superintendent of an apartment building. They divorced in Escambia County in August of 1958. She died in May of 2003, and is buried In Bayview Memorial Park.

Eulalie Turner Moore, Henry's widow, married Lewis Kenneth Cahn in May of 1941, and died March 21, 1982. Henry Hicks Moore, Jr. was only 2 years old when his father was killed. He grew up to be a prominent citizen in Pensacola, and was a community activist who wrote many opinion pieces for the News Journal. He died on December 26, 2010. He was an interesting person, and a google search should be productive for those interested.

I doubt this case, and the Hinote-Bryars murders from 1931 were connected. The crime scenes were not too far apart, but there was no attempt to assault Miss Gregory. I think it was just a robbery gone wrong. When Miss Gregory screamed, she may have startled one of the robbers into accidently firing his weapon. According to her, they didn't stick around after that and took nothing.

Chapter Seven

The Curious Murder of Charles E. Sudmall

Charles E. Sudmall may be remembered locally as the man who built our Exchange Hotel in Milton, and the manager of the West Florida Telephone, and Telegraph company. There is much more to his story, however. Sudmall immigrated to the U.S. from Dundag, Russia, (present day, Latvia) in 1895 when he was 20, or 21 years old. The Massachusetts State and Federal Naturalization records state that he arrived on the tenth of June, 1895. He signed a Declaration to denounce Tsar Nicholas of Russia, and become a citizen of the United States. A passport application in 1912 stated that he arrived from Buenos Aires in June of 1895 aboard the ship, Angara. The application stated that he lived in Boston, New Port, Rhode Island, Pensacola, and Milton, residing in the U.S. for 16 years.

    By 1898, he was living in Pensacola on South Palafox, and working as a "bayman", which is defined as a person who fishes the bay. In just a few years, however, he was living in Milton, and listed his occupation as an electrician. By 1906, he was living in Milton and was the manager of the Milton Telephone Exchange, and in September of that year, he was charged with the murder of an attorney named Lawrence N. Ervin. According to newspaper accounts, he and Ervin were having dinner, and Ervin felt insulted over something that was said. He demanded an apology, and Sudmall refused and left the scene to walk over to a livery stable. Ervin followed him and once again demanded an apology. Sudmall again refused and walked away, this time to the phone exchange building, where he went to the second-floor balcony and sat down. About 30 minutes later, Ervin appeared and cursing, once again demanded an apology. This time when Sudmall refused, Ervin produced a knife, and cut Sudmall at least two times. Sudmall then struck Ervin in the face causing him to fall off of the balcony, and fracturing his skull on the street below. Ervin died about 10 days later. (He is buried in DeFuniak Springs).

Represented by future Attorney-General Thomas F. West, Sudmall was exonerated during a hearing with Judge Holley due to self-defense.

Sudmall did become a naturalized citizen in Pensacola in June of 1911. His passport application describes him as: 5'9" tall; prominent forehead; hazel eyes; prominent "Greek" nose, medium mouth, and chin; dark hair with olive complexion, and a rather large face. He left the country and went back to Russia to visit his family for a few months.

He registered for the draft in September 1918, showing his occupation as "Telephone Manager". In the 1919 publication, The American Telephone Journal, he is described as the General Manager of the Gulf Telephone and Telegraph company at Milton. He had been in the business for 13 years and had 200 subscribers. Before getting into the business, he had worked at the Pensacola Navy Yard in the electrical department. He was a member of the Florida Telephone Association.

Charles Sudmall was a pretty wealthy man by the time the '20s rolled around. Not only did he own the Telephone exchange in Milton, but he owned the Marianna Telephone Exchange, the Exchange Hotel, and a hotel in Floridatown. He had no family in the United States. He never married, and seemed focused on his businesses and becoming successful. One of his business partners in Milton was Grover Cleveland (Cleve) Harvell, the son of the former local Sheriff, James Harvell. Cleve Harvell and Sudmall were partners in a garage in town, and Harvell was also an agent for Star Automobiles.

A Very Suspicious Killing

On the last morning of his life, Charles Sudmall's conversation with Cleve Harvell was partially overheard by Mr. Falk, (or maybe, Faulk) who owned the Santa Rosa Hotel. Falk was at the garage to pay a bill and heard Sudmall ask Harvell if he was going to be busy. Harvell said he was going to Pensacola but would see him on his return. Falk later testified that the conversation seemed friendly.

Culver W. Cobb later testified that he, Harvell, and H.C. Collins took a trip to Pensacola the day of the killing. Harvell had a .32 caliber pistol, and he had fired it from the ferry as they were returning. Cobb said this pistol was the same one found next to Sudmall's body later that evening.

About 7:20 pm, Mrs. Hinote, the night operator at the phone exchange received a call from Harvell looking for Sudmall. She transferred the call to the hotel and waited on the line for Sudmall to answer. She heard Harvell say, "Well, I got back." Sudmall said, "Who is this"? "Cleve." "I'll be right down" Sudmall said. He then stopped by his office and got something from his desk and put it in his pocket. Lillie Nelson said she saw him do this 6, or 7 minutes before the shooting.

Apparently, when Sudmall reached the garage, there was an immediate sound of gunfire. Cleve Harvell, and Walton C. Rhoades, (sometimes referred to as Walter), were the only ones in the garage when Sudmall entered. C.W. Cobb claimed that he and another man were the first to reach the garage after the shooting, and were let into the building by Rhoades. He testified that a pistol found next to Sudmall's body was the same one Harvell was displaying earlier in the day. He also claimed that Harvell walked him to the back of the garage, and requested that he not identify the pistol as belonging to him.

Luther Fisher, undertaker, examined Sudmall's body later that evening. He found eight bullet wounds; five in the body, one in the leg, and two in the arm. He testified that Harvell, who was a close friend of his, admitted that both he and Rhoades had shot Sudmall. Fisher said the killing was planned and premeditated. Rhoades was instructed to hide in the corner and shoot Sudmall as soon as he entered the garage. Rhoades missed the first two shots, but then hit him three times. Harvell hit him with five shots. Harvell then claimed that Sudmall was his best friend in Milton and that Rhoades had killed him. He asked Fisher to say that the body only had five bullet wounds. L. Douglas Wolfe, an assistant of Fisher's, (and later owner of the Wolfe Funeral Home), testified that while he was preparing Sudmall's body and sewing up the bullet holes, someone asked how many bullet holes there were and Harvell spoke up and said, "There ain't more than five, are there?" and winked his eyes at

Wolfe. Supposedly Harvell was drunk at the time, but other witnesses claimed he was sober.

State Attorney Thompson's case was that:

- Harvell, and Sudmall were in business together.
- Harvell called Sudmall over the phone to come to the garage.
- Sudmall was shot as he entered the building.
- Sudmall's body had two different kinds of bullets in it.
- Eight bullets entered his body.
- Only Rhoades, and Harvell were waiting in the garage.
- The pistol found by Sudmall belonged to Harvell.

The defense claimed self-defense, and Rhoades took all the blame for the killing. The first trial of the two in the spring ended in a mistrial. After the mistrial, attorneys for Harvell, and Rhoades filed a writ of Habeas Corpus with the Florida Supreme Court and got them released on $5000 bail until they were retried. On October 3, 1924, after a retrial, Harvell was acquitted and Rhoades was "Nol Prossed". They dropped prosecution on Rhoades.

This whole case stinks. Remember, Charles Sudmall was a very wealthy, successful man with no family ties in the United States. In December 1923, County Judge H. W. Thompson, appointed Culver W. Cobb, (yes, the same one who testified at the Harvell trial), as Curator of Sudmall's estate. Sudmall's Last Will and Testament was written and witnessed in May of 1910. The original executor that Sudmall requested had passed away, so the vacancy was filled by Cobb. I believe Thompson is the same State Attorney who led the prosecution of Harvell, and Rhoades.

Listed in the inventory of Sudmall's possessions were seven automobiles:

- Ford Touring Car 1917 model
- Ford Touring Car 1923 model
- Cole Eight Touring car
- Willys-Knight Touring car, model 64. Serial #28860, motor #76600
- New Overland Red Bird Car model 92, Ser #11065, motor #92-16419
- New Overland Touring car model 91, Ser # 49460, motor #52367
- Another Overland Touring car model 91, Ser # 49372, motor# 52708

    I am thinking the cars were part of the inventory for sale in the business Sudmall owned with Harvell. I would like to know, but so far haven't been able to find out what happened to the cars. Supposedly they were to be sold with the proceeds going to the estate. I wonder who ended up with them, and at what price.

    Culver W. Cobb was born in April 1890, and his father was Farrar H. Cobb. C. W. was a cashier at the First National Bank in Milton.

    After Sudmall was killed, the West Florida Telephone, and Telegraph Company met in Marianna, and selected a new President. Peter L. Rosasco was made President, and R.A. McGeachy a director. McGeachy was a Milton Attorney.

    At some point, Peter Rosasco was made Administrator of Sudmall's estate. In October of 1927, Arthur B. Lule, Solicitor General of Latvia, requested Rosasco be removed from his role. The request was granted by Judge McLeod. Mr. Rule was acting at the request of Charles Sudmall's father Karl and he was charging a "misappropriation, or misapplication of funds."

    What a tangled web it was. I believe that there was a plot to do away with this foreigner who had become successful in this country, and divide his wealth. Of course, a jury in Santa Rosa County was going to acquit a well-known local boy of killing someone from Russia.

Whatever Happened to….

Cleve Harvell died 12 June 1974, and is buried at Ft. Barrancas National Cemetery. On his WWI draft registration card, it states that he is a Chief Deputy Sheriff. He served in the U.S. Army from 9 Nov 1917 to 7 Dec 1918. In 1921 he married Ruby Wiggins. In 1925 They lived in Tallahassee and he was the Manager of the M.A. Houston Motor Company.

Walton Canvass Rhoades was born in 1879. In the 1910 census for Santa Rosa County, he is listed as a Druggist. In the 1909 fire that burned most of downtown Milton, he lost his drug store. Shortly after he reopened in the Wiggins building.

He married Nancy Charity Hilton in Milton on 23 Aug 1903, and in the 1920 census she is listed as a Hotel Proprietor. I was unable to find him listed in 1920.

In 1929 He, and his wife were living in Miami, and he was in the Produce business.

In 1930 he was living in Pahokee, Palm Beach County, Fl, and listed as a grower, and buyer for fruits and vegetables, while his wife and daughter were in Knoxville, Tenn. Working at the LeConte Hotel.

In 1934, Nan was shown as the Manager of the Bay Court Apartments in Miami.

It looks like they stayed in the Miami area until he passed away in 1937, and she died in 1959. They are both buried in the Woodlawn Park North Cemetery in Miami.

Charles E. Sudmall

Chapter Eight

Statewide Pursuit and Capture of Criminals Near Milton

In March of 1931, four wanted desperadoes on a state-wide crime spree were captured by a posse comprised of police officers, and citizens from different Panhandle communities. After spending the night in hiding in the Mulat swamp, six miles west of Milton, the trapped criminals surrendered to Deputy Sheriff Wade Cobb of Milton, Deputy Alex Cooper of Washington county, and Roscoe Rollins, a civilian from Chipley.

The quartet on the run were two men, Leonard "Tex" Hayes, Bert Oglesby, and two women, Fay Harris, and Mabel Wertz. The women were from St. Louis, Missouri, and the men from Oklahoma.

The crime spree started in Jacksonville on Wednesday night, March 4, when two police officers recognized an Oklahoma license plate reported to be on a car used in a hold up on Feb. 25th. Officer Wilbur Blizzard was shot, and patrolman H. V. Branch was clubbed. The bandits fled to the west and abandoned their car at Lake City.

Early Thursday morning, they seized a truck in Wellborn, Florida, twenty miles west of Lake City, and took two hostages, father and son, D.C., and J. L. McDonald. They continued westward with their hostages two hundred miles to Chipley. Officers in Chipley had been forewarned by authorities in Live Oak that the bandits were probably heading their way, and were on the lookout for them.

Nearing Chipley, the bandits were engaged in a gun battle with the local officers badly wounding Posse man Gillis Malloy, and Deputy D. J. Brock, who were later transported to a hospital in Dothan, Alabama. Both eventually recovered, even though Malloy was hit at least 6 times. There were also 40 convicts, and their guards who were near the shootout and ordered to lie down by the bandits. The quartet seized a car from a motorist and headed back to the east for seven miles, before taking another car, and eventually turning back to the west. The McDonalds got away from them during the gun fight, and were not injured. One of the male bandits was using a "riot" gun, and one of the women was using a small automatic pistol, and Deputy Brock believed (mistakenly) that he had hit her with one shot.

There were reports coming in from all over with the bandits being spotted heading to Panama City, Dothan, Ala., and Pensacola. Later, it was learned that after taking a car from a motorist, the bandits sped east to Cottondale, turned off on a side road and went north, then got back on the main road to DeFuniak Springs where they obtained eight gallons of gasoline and continued on toward Pensacola.

The bandit car was seen speeding across the Blackwater River bridge into Milton, and the final pursuit began. Deputy Sheriff Wade Cobb, Mack Williams, and other citizens, including the Mayor of Chipley, R. H. Rollins, and Deputy Alex Cooper from Washington County, gave chase and the bandits turned off the main road at the Rozier farm, and after three miles on the backroad abandoned their car and went into the marsh on foot. A perimeter was set up and the bandits spent the night in the swamp.

Recognizing the hopelessness of their situation the four surrendered, with Mabel Wertz shouting, "Don't shoot, we're coming out!" As they came out Hayes made a move like he might be reaching for a gun, but Deputy Cobb had him covered with an automatic rifle. Wertz had a handbag under her arm and unsuccessfully tried to prevent the deputies from taking it. Hayes, and Oglesby were disarmed and a rifle was found in the woods. The only wounds noted on the bandits were a slight cut on Oglesby's ear, probably caused by a flying piece of glass in the Chipley shoot-out.

Santa Rosa County Sheriff Henry Mitchell, and Escambia County Sheriff Mose Penton were attending the state Sheriff's convention at Sarasota. They drove all night Thursday, and arrived in Milton Friday morning. The prisoners posed for photographs, and answered some questions from a Gazette reporter.

The prisoners were transported back to Washington county Friday afternoon, and formally charged with highway robbery, assault with intent to murder, and kidnapping.

A large crowd had gathered in Chipley when the convoy of three cars arrived, and it was thought that an attempt would be made against the men who had shot and wounded the two Washington county posse men. There was no attempt. Sheriffs Mitchell, and Sheriff Farrior of Washington county appeared in front of the crowd at the courthouse and talked to the assembled crowd. Sheriff Mitchell described the events, and complemented Sheriff Farrior for his assistance, then appealed for the crowd to go home and let the law take its course. He received a large round of applause.

By Monday, Sheriff Mitchell received letters, and photographs from Tulsa, Oklahoma, and Dallas, Texas, and other places. A detective from Tulsa, Jack Bonham, was particularly interested to know if Mabel Wertz, who was also known as Dammerel, was still with Oglesby. Bonham said that Wertz was from a nice family in St. Louis, but had married a criminal named Doc Dammerel, who was now serving time in the Oklahoma Penitentiary for highway robbery. Oglesby was wanted in Oklahoma for escaping from the State Prison. According to a letter found on Wertz, she was the mother of two children. The letter was from her mother, begging her to give up her association with Oglesby, and come home to the children.

Hayes, and Oglesby had escaped from jail in Springfield Missouri, by taking a gun from a jailor and forcing him to open the outside door of the jail. As they escaped the jailor fired a rifle at the escapees, hitting Hayes and another escapee in the neck, and Oglesby in the shoulder. Detective Bonham in his letter, said that Wertz had smuggled in the gun for the jailbreak. A car that was stolen by the escapees was abandoned in Tulsa, Oklahoma.

Sheriff Marcel Hendrix of Green County, Springfield, Missouri, was anxious to get Hayes and Oglesby. They were wanted for numerous robberies in Missouri, and Oklahoma, and for breaking out of jail in Springfield on January 27th. Sheriff Mitchell received the following telegram from the Springfield Sheriff Friday night:

"See you have Burt Oglesby, Tex Hayes, Mabel Dammerel alias Mabel Wertz and Fay Harris. I am much interested in the capture of these men as they and four others broke out of jail here January 27th.

One of their partners recaptured and sentenced to 40 years today, and another got twenty-five years. If you do not have a strong case, I am anxious for these men. Positive they will receive Ninety-nine here. Will extradite."

Sheriff Mitchell informed the Missouri officials that the prisoners had already been turned over to Washington County.

Hayes, and Oglesby were indicted as principals, and Wertz, and Harris as accessories. All four pled not guilty to the charges in front of Circuit Court Judge C. D. Jones. States attorney L. V. McRae said all four would be tried jointly. None of the four displayed any anxiety over being held for trial.

On April 2, 1931 after changing their pleas to guilty, Hayes, and Oglesby were sentenced to 20 years for robbery and 10 years with assault with intent to commit murder. The sentences were to run concurrently. The two women were sentenced to 10 years for being accessories to the robberies, and to five years for being accessories to the assaults. Judge Jones denied the couple's request to be married before sending them to prison.

At the time of his arrest, Bert Oglesby was on parole from an eight-year sentence for car theft, and burglary in Oklahoma. Governor Murray revoked the parole upon learning of the Florida crime spree. C.E.B. Culter, a pardon, and parole attorney, said there would be no attempt to return Oglesby to Oklahoma if he was prosecuted in Florida.

In October of 1931, Oglesby's brother Jack, 22, and his sister Zelma M. Woodmansee, attempted to mail arms, and ammunition to Oglesby at the prison in Starke, FL. Mrs. J. Young, Postmistress, at Starke, 12 miles from the prison, testified that she had received a package containing two pistols mailed from Tulsa. Oglesby, and Woodmansee pleaded not guilty when arraigned and were released on $5000 bond. They were later found guilty, and sentenced to prison.

The two women, who had become known as the "bobbed-hair bandits", were paroled from the state prison in Raiford on November 27, 1935. They were released on December 22nd, to the county judge in Tulsa, Oklahoma. The length of their parole was for six months. They were eligible for a full pardon after their parole completed.

Bert Oglesby died in prison of pneumonia and Typhoid on July 2, 1932, and his body was shipped back to Tulsa, Oklahoma.

Mabel Wertz Dammerel died in Los Angeles, California in March of 1952, and is buried in the same North Hollywood cemetery where Curly Joe of Three Stooges fame, and the wrestler Gorgeous George are buried. No further information could be found on Tex Hayes, or Fay Harris.

From The Milton Gazette

Chapter Nine

The Edwards Murders
Mulat
June 29, 1951

    Lawrence Cormack, 22, was awaiting transfer to Raiford for a 10-year sentence for the burglary of a Milton Grocery store that he committed with his 16-year-old brother, Neal. Lawrence escaped from the county jail in Milton on Friday morning, 29 June, and stole a .32 caliber revolver from the car belonging to Santa Rosa County Deputy Clyde Murphy.

    Julian Edwards, 75, and his wife Mae, 73 lived just south of the L&N railroad track in Mulat. Around 11:30 pm, Cormack entered their house, and using the stolen revolver, shot and killed the elderly couple in their bed. Mr. Edwards was shot 5 times, and his wife once through the back with the bullet piercing her heart. The black leather holster for the stolen revolver was found the next day about 50 yards away from the house.

    Ernest Edwards, the slain couple's son, lived about 200 yards away. He said he heard shots fired around 11:30, and went outside of his house to quiet the dogs down. He rose early the next morning to do chores, and discovered the bodies of his parents about 8 am.

    A large posse was formed in Milton, with the intention of finding Cormack. He was an immediate suspect, especially with the discovery of the holster identified as belonging with the stolen revolver.

    About 7 am the jailer, Steve Stephens, found Cormack sleeping in the Circuit Judge's office. He alerted Deputy Murphy, and Cormack was taken into custody without a fight. He claimed that with everyone looking for him, the courthouse seemed a safe place to hide.

Cormack Background

Lawrence Cormack was only seven years old the first time he was sent to a reform school. His father was an abusive drunk, and he later stated that his mother was deaf, and really did not provide a stable home. He did not remember the reason he was sent away, but that he did run away from home more than once. By the time he was a teenager, he had been arrested for petty theft, breaking and entering, car theft, and mail theft.

He went to Wichita as a teenager and was picked up for vagrancy. He then went to California and joined the Merchant Marine. He was caught opening packages that were on their way to servicemen serving in the Philippines. He was sentenced to 5 years in an Army stockade, and fined $2000. When released he found his way to San Diego where he was arrested on a burglary charge. He was sent to reformatory in Lancaster, California for 15 months. Soon arrested again for auto theft, he was sent to prison in El Reno, Oklahoma where he was released after 19 months for good behavior. He spent Christmas at home, and then joined the Army. After six months of training, he was sent to a school for cooks, and bakers from where he deserted a week later. He went to San Francisco to stay with an uncle where he stole his car, (possibly a 1950 Nash), and returned home to Bird City, Kansas. He was joined by his 16-year-old brother Neal and committed numerous burglaries in Bird City, and stole license plates in the Kansas City area.

After making their way to Milton, they broke into the Jitney Jungle and stole $71. While sleeping in the woods near DeFuniak Springs they were taken into custody when a farmer reported suspicious characters to the local police department.

Lawrence took the blame for the burglaries, and his brother Neal was shipped back home. He was sentenced to 10 years in the state prison at Raiford, and was awaiting transportation when he escaped.

Cormack escaped the jail by hiding when the prisoners were being returned to their cells after a work detail of scrubbing part of the building. He hid and the jailer did not miss him. He sneaked into the grand jury room of the courthouse and watched from a window until Sheriff Hayes, and Deputy Cobb left for the day. He then tried to steal Murphy's car but couldn't hotwire it, but he did take a .32 caliber pistol and shells from the glove compartment.

Cormack's account of the murders.

Cormack stated that after escaping, he hid out most of the day before looking for food. I think he followed the railroad track from the courthouse until he arrived at the Mulat area and saw the Edwards home. Leaving his shoes and socks with the leather holster, he entered the house through a window and was rifling through Mr. Edwards' pants pockets when Edwards woke up and confronted him. He panicked, and began shooting. Mrs. Edwards was shot while trying to help her husband against the intruder.

Cormack fled the scene, leaving his shoes, socks, and the holster. He stopped at the wayside park on Pond Creek and highway 90 and threw the gun in the water. Then he walked to the courthouse and hid in the second-floor office of the Circuit Judge. He slept there until discovered by the jailer.

There were two different trials for the two murders. It was felt that he could not get a fair trial in Santa Rosa County, so a change of venue was granted and the trials were held in Escambia County. Cormack was found guilty of first-degree murder in both trials, and sentenced to two life terms. After only 20 years in prison, he was paroled, but violated the terms of his parole when he traveled to New York City. He turned himself in back in Jacksonville two years later, and was returned to prison. In December of 1978, he was nearing another parole date, when he escaped from the minimum-security camp after stealing $1700 from the prison canteen. He was recaptured about 9 miles away in Stark, Florida while walking along Highway 301.

I haven't found when he was released for good from prison, but he died in Jacksonville, in November 1993.

The Pensacola Journal

Milton Gazette

July 5, 1951

Transcript of Cormack's confession to Woodrow Melvin, Santa Rosa County Attorney.

Statement taken at the Santa Rosa County jail, Milton, Florida, July 1, 1951 at 11 pm.

Mr. Cormack, I am Woodrow Melvin. I am the County Attorney for Santa Rosa County. The lady who is taking down your testimony is Miss Marguerite Williams. The gentleman sitting next to her is Mr. Clayton Mapoles, the editor of The Milton Gazette. The gentleman sitting next to him is Sheriff Marshall Hayes, Sheriff of Santa Rosa County. The gentleman standing just behind Mr. Hayes is Mr. Wade Cobb who is a Deputy Sheriff of Santa Rosa County. The gentleman standing just behind me is Mr. Hilson Crawford.

Q- Your name is Lawrence William Cormack?
A- Yes, sir.

Q- Lawrence, I understand that you would like to make a statement concerning the details in connection with the death of Mr. and Mrs. Julian C. Edwards, Is that correct?
A- Yes, sir.

Q- Have I, or the Sheriff, or the Deputy Sheriffs, or anyone offered you any reward for making this statement or are you making it freely and voluntarily?
A- I am making it freely and voluntarily.

Q- You realize that this statement made by you could be used as evidence should the State of Florida prosecute you?
A- Yes, sir.

Q- Lawrence, I would like for you to start at the beginning and talk slowly so that Miss Williams can write it down and tell us whatever it is you want to tell us about what happened after you left the Santa Rosa County jail last Thursday night, June 28th. June 28th is the night you got out of the Santa Rosa County jail, Is that right?
A- Yes, sir.

Q- After you left the Courthouse what happened, Mr. Cormack?
A- I got in the car down there and there wasn't any keys in there nor nothing. I went in the glove compartment looking for keys and found a box of shells and gun. I tried to wire the car but couldn't so I took the gun and shells with me. I went over to the green Ford and there was a key in the glove compartment but it wouldn't work so I beat it. I went up the street, I don't know what the name of it was. I went out the highway, walked three or four miles until daylight Friday morning, then I went back in the woods and tried to sleep but ants and mosquitoes were too bad and I went back to the road. I come on to the creek, went swimming in it and I laid down and went to sleep and it was after dark when I woke up Friday night. I tied my clothes in a bundle and waded the creek until I come to a place where there was an empty house and I crossed the road and I come to this house and sit down there and left the scabbard to the gun.

Q- You left the scabbard where?
A- Where I was sitting.

Q- Now you are speaking of the scabbard and gun you got from the car. Was the gun a rifle or what kind of gun?
A- A .32 pistol. I left the scabbard outside and in front of the house. Then I crossed over to the gate, took off my shoes, went up on the porch.

Q- Did you take your socks off?
A- I took them off.

Q- What happened?
A- I went in the kitchen, got a drink of water then I went to the bedroom by the bathroom and I was going to get this man's money and I seen what looked like his clothes on a stool in the bedroom. Just as I went through the door the man sit up and said something like, "Get the hell out of here." It scared me and I pulled the gun out of my pocket and started shooting.

Q- Did his wife get out of bed?
A- No, sir, she sat up in the line of fire and said, "Who is that shooting." I turned around and ran out the way I come in and somebody turned on the light in the bedroom when I ran out the back door, so I run on down the road. I walked until I come to the crossroads, turned left there, and went to the back door of a house and got a drink from a pump and went on down the highway. From the highway I went down to the park and sit around there.

Q- You went to the park, did you say?
A- Yes, sir.

Q- Is that park about a mile west of Milton on the highway?
A- Yes, sir. I sat around there for a while, drank some water and thought about shooting myself in the head with the gun—then backed out. In the meantime, I loaded the gun again and threw it in the water.

Q- You threw it in the water. You threw it from the bank or the bridge?

A- From the bridge.

Q- From which side?
A-It was on the right side coming toward Milton. I took the shells out of my pocket and threw them in also. I walked back to Milton and I was I Milton a little after daylight. I was going to turn myself in and I got scared and stayed in the County Commissioner's room most of the day and slipped to the back of the Courtroom and laid on the back benches, then I went in the room where I thought there was an X-ray machine.

Q- Lawrence, did you stay in the room where the machine in until after dark?
A- I stayed in the Courtroom until after dark.

Q- When did you change over to the room where the jailer found you/
A- About 12:00 o'clock.

Q- That was Saturday night, last night, that you speak of having spent here in the Courthouse in Milton, particularly from 12:00 o'clock midnight until you woke up?
A- Yes, sir.

Q- Did you leave out of the Courthouse building from the time you entered a little after daylight Saturday morning?
A- No, sir.

Q- In other words, you didn't leave the Courthouse building from the time you entered a little after daylight Saturday morning?
A- That's right.

Q- Lawrence, let's go back now a little bit. When you came up to this house in which you later killed the man and his wife on the bed, I believe you said, what did you say you had in mind when you went in the house?

A- I was going in to get some money. I thought about getting some food and decided I would make too much noise because I couldn't see my way around in the kitchen.

Q- You went in the building, rather dwelling house, for the purpose of committing a robbery?
A- Yes, sir.

Q- Now, can you tell us how many times you shot the man who raised up in bed?
A- No, sir.

Q- Did you keep shooting them until the gun ran out of bullets?
A- Yes, sir.

Q- Did you snap the gun after it was empty?
A- Yes, sir.

Q- You didn't attempt to reload the pistol after you fired it out?
A- No, sir.

Q- The light that turned on—was it in the room Mr. and Mrs. Edwards were in or was it in a different room?
A- In the same room.

Q- Apparently either she or he turned the light on?
A- I was about one-half way out when the screen door slammed. Sounded like the screen door.

Q- But they turned the light on?
A- They turned the light on.

Q- When you snapped the gun empty were you shooting at the man or the woman?
A- I don't remember.

Q- Did you walk around at the foot of the bed and shoot either of them?
A- No, sir.

Q- You did all of the shooting from the inside leading from the inside of the bedroom?
A- Yes, sir.

Q- Lawrence, you know that you had the gun loaded when you went in the house?
A- Yes, sir; it had five shells in it when I got it and I put another one in it on the first night.

Q- You know that you unloaded the gun on Mr. and Mrs. Edwards in the bedroom?
A- Yes, sir.

Q- Now, when you left, you left your shoes inside the gate—the same place you left them when you went in the house?
A- Yes, sir.

Q- What kind of socks were you wearing?
A- Army tan.

Q- Do you remember if they had size 11 stamped on them?
A- Yes, sir, they did.

Q- Then, these socks and shoes are yours?
A- Yes, sir.

Q- Has the Sheriff carried you back to the house?
A- Yes, sir.

Q- Is the house you went in the same house you were in when you killed those people?

A- Yes, sir.

Q- Do you know whether this was in Santa Rosa County?
A- (Unknown)

Q- Did you go in the same room with the Sheriff as you went in and shot those people?
A- Yes, sir.

Q- Did you see the blood stains on the bed?
A- Yes, sir.

Q- You recognized that place as being the place where you had been?
A- Yes, sir.

Q- Since the Jailer found you yesterday morning sleeping in the Judge's office, has anyone mistreated you in any way, Lawrence?
A- No, sir.

Q- You have talked to the State Attorney?
A- Yes, sir.

Q- Did he mistreat or abuse you in any way?
A- No, sir.

Q- Did Sheriff Hayes mistreat or abuse you in any way?
A- No, sir.

Q- Did Deputy Sheriff Wade Cobb mistreat or abuse you in any way?
A-No, sir

Q- How about Mr. Harvell Enfinger?
A- No, sir.

Q- Have you been treated just as nice by the Sheriff and his force since you were taken back Sunday morning as you had been treated before you got out Thursday night?
A- Yes, sir.

Q- None of them have promised you that they would talk to the Judge for you or get you any consideration?
A- No, sir.

Q- By "no sir" you mean that none of them have promised you anything?
A- Yes, sir.

Q- Lawrence, is there anything else you would like for her to write down?
A- That's about all.

Q- When you took your shoes off at the gate that was so you could go in quietly and come back and pick them up?
A- Yes, sir, but when I heard that door slam, I thought someone was after me and I run on down the road without them.

Q- You were out in the yard when you took your shoes off?
A- Yes, sir.

Q- Had you already decided to rob who ever lived in there?
A- Yes, sir.

Q- Did you see anyone moving around in the house while you were sitting outside?
A- No, sir.

Q- Did you know who lived there?
A- No, sir.

Q- At the time you saw cars on the highway would you jump out in the woods and hide?

A- Yes, sir.

Q- Did you see the Sheriff's car going down there?
A- No, sir.

Q- No, at that time you were back here.

Q- Lawrence, as you walked back from the Edwards' house barefooted, what did that do to your feet?
A- I got a blister on one foot.

Q- Which foot?
A- Left foot.

Q- On the instep of your left foot?
A- Right on the ball.

Q- Did you notice any blood on your clothes?
A- No, sir.

Q- Mr. and Mrs. Edwards' son lived just below them, about 200 yards. Did you notice a light on in this house, or did you know there was a house down below?
A- No, sir. I didn't know there was a house there and didn't see a light.

Q- You do know that a light was turned on in the house, which you left, immediately after you left.
A- That was the reason I left my shoes.

Q- The pistol that you used to shoot Mr. and Mrs. Edwards with—Is that the same pistol that you took from Mr. Clyde Murphy's car?
A- Yes, sir.

Mr. Melvin—Will all of you please go outside the room and leave just the three of us.

Q- Now, Lawrence, there is no one in here except you, and I and Miss Williams. I just want to ask you again if the statement that you have made has been made by you freely and voluntarily?
A- Yes, sir.

Q- No one has promised you anything to get it?
A- No, sir.

Q- You realize that the statement you have just made can be used as evidence against you? Realizing this, you do re-affirm and tell me that all you have told is the truth?
A- Yes, sir.

Q- When you were first questioned today by the Sheriff or by the State Attorney, when did you tell them that you came back to the courthouse?
A- About 12:00 o'clock Friday night.

Q- Did you tell them that you had been in the County Courtroom or building until you were found this Sunday morning?
A- Yes, sir.

Q- When did you finally decide to make the statement that you made here this evening?
A- About 7:00 o'clock when I was talking to Mr. Crawford.

Q- You decided to make the statement. Did Mr. Crawford promise you anything?
A- No, sir.

Q- Was it that you had your mind burdened and wanted to get it off your mind?
A- Yes, sir.

Q- Did you tell Mr. Crawford that you wanted to make the statement?
A- Yes, sir.

July 2, 1951, typing at this point started at 10:23 pm. I have read the foregoing six and one-half pages of the statement and I hereby state the statement was made freely and voluntarily in answer to questions as listed on these pages in the exact wording as typed except for the correction I made on page 4. I had previously been advised that I did not have to make statement and that any statement that I might make could and might be used against me in Court, and that under the Constitution of the United States and of the State of Florida that I did not have to make any statement, that I was entitled to have an attorney and to talk to an attorney, and that any statement that I made or gave would have to be made freely and voluntarily made and that I did make the statement and do now sign the same as my statement concerning this case and the happenings as set forth herein as being a true and correct statement of what happened and as my free and voluntary statement.

LAWRENCE W. CORMACK
Witnesses:
MARSHALL HAYES, Sheriff
WADE A COBB.

MR. AND MRS. JULIAN C. EDWARDS, elderly couple, were slain Friday night in their bedroom of this Mulat home. Lawrence W. Cormack, convict who had escaped from Santa Rosa county jail the previous night, confessed the shooting after being taken into custody Sunday morning. Cormack shot the couple after entering their home in a robbery attempt, he told county officers.

From The Milton Gazette

Mae Edwards

Julian Edwards

Chapter Ten

The Tragic Death of Big Ed Morris

Big Ed Morris got into a fight one night on the bank of Little Escambia creek, and died in the hospital in Century, Florida three days later. This is his story.

Walter Edward Morris was born in Foshee, Alabama on 7 December 1899. His mother was Ella Morris, and it is believed that his father was a sawmill operator known as Captain Fuller. The 1900 census for Owen, Escambia Co, Alabama lists a Levander Fuller, born in North Carolina in 1859. Ella, and her two children, Edward, and Stella were living with her mother, Cornelia Morris, who kept a boarding house, and her four brothers. In the 1910, and 1920 census, Ella and her children were still living in Owen. There is no more sign of Mr. Fuller.

In the 1920 census Ed is listed as a laborer but he already had a reputation as a talented up-and -coming pitcher on the local baseball scene. In 1919 and part of 1920 he played for the Bagdad team, and pitched for the Century, Fla. Town club when he was signed by the Class-D Bradenton Growers of the Florida State League.

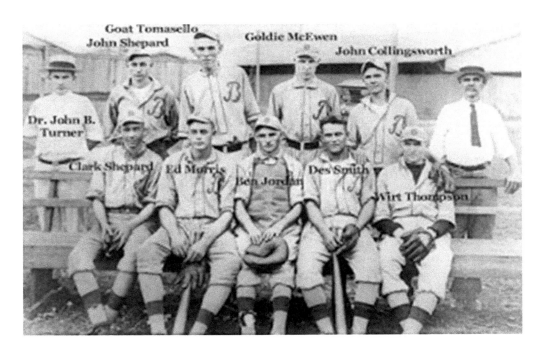

The Bagdad Baseball Club, 1920-1922

Morris toiled in the minor leagues until 1928, with only a brief call -up to the Chicago Cubs in 1922, where he got 12 innings of work. In the spring training of 1925, he got a tryout with the Cincinnati Reds but was returned to the Nashville team with a sore arm. Ed had developed the reputation for being a hard drinker, who really made no effort at conditioning, or taking care of himself.

In 1928, Morris got his big break with the hapless Boston Red Sox. He took full advantage of his opportunity, and won his first start on May 3 with a 4-hit victory over the Philadelphia Athletics. Through the 25th of August his record was 17-11 with an era of 3.13. Stellar numbers for sure, but possibly the length of the season wore him down. He finished 19-15 with a 3.53 era. He also had pitched 257 innings. His record was still the best among rookie pitchers, and his 19 victories accounted for a third of the Red Sox wins that year.

In 1929, Morris suffered arm problems and other nagging injuries that resulted in a season record of 14 wins and 14 losses. He pitched 208 innings and had a 4.45 era. During the winter before the season, Morris had traveled to the Panama Canal region, and found a team that wanted to hire him to pitch. Morris wired Baseball Commissioner Judge Kennesaw Mountain Landis for permission to pitch. Landis wired back that permission could not be granted due to rules prohibiting major league ballplayers from playing for money during the offseason. Morris pitched a couple of games anyway, defeating the Navy fleet team 4-3, and becoming a hero in the Canal Zone. In March during spring training Landis fined him $250. It was considered lucky that Morris was not also handed a suspension. There is one notable game from 1929. On 26 May, Morris pitched against the Yankees. The game ended in a 15-4 blowout for the victorious Yanks, and Morris was largely ineffective. He gave up a three-run homer to Yankee catcher Bill Dickey, and a double to Lou Gehrig, but in the fifth inning Big Ed Morris hit a home run off of Waite Hoyt to tie the game 3-3. At the conclusion of the inning Hoyt was walking toward the Yankee dugout and said something to the umpire, and got ejected from the game. It was Morris' only major league home run.

The 1930 season started with spring training at Pensacola's Legion Field, with the players staying at the San Carlos Hotel. Morris was a holdout for a short time demanding a raise. He settled for a $500 raise to a season salary of $8000. The Red Sox considered Morris to be the Ace of their pitching staff for the upcoming season. The New York Yankees had made a strong effort to obtain Morris during the offseason. Once again, he developed arm problems and missed the second half of the season. His record was 4-9 with a 4.13 era.

After the 1930 season, Morris had a house built in Flomaton, Alabama, and moved his family there from Mobile. He had a wife, Beryl, and two sons, Edward, and Mortimer by this time, and they lived there until his death.

1931 was, once again, a season of a sore arm. Morris also missed three weeks in May after being hit on his big toe during batting practice by a line drive hit by outfielder Tom Oliver. He was sent home from Philadelphia to Boston to get treatment. He started to improve late in the season, but finished with 5 wins and 7 losses with a 4.75 era. His dismal record was the result of "injuries, and failure to condition". His last appearance was a complete game 4-hit victory, 9-2 over the St. Louis Browns. He and the Red Sox were looking forward to 1932 as comeback season.

> Flomaton had the largest funeral in the memory of many aged residents when Morris was buried. Tommy Oliver, teammate of Morris, came from Savannah to represent the Boston club at the services.

Pensacola Journal 12 March 1932

A Going Away Fish Fry

The 1932 spring training for the Red Sox was to be in Savannah, Georgia. To celebrate the new season, and a new contract for Morris, there was to be a fish fry/peanut boil to be held in his honor. This was held on Little Escambia Creek between Flomaton, and Brewton, Alabama on 29 Feb 1932. At some point during the evening there was an altercation between Morris and a Brewton filling station operator named Joe White. Morris knocked White down, and then he tripped and fell on top of him. White stabbed him twice in the chest with his pocket knife. An L&N railroad employee named Dixon was cut when he was attempting to break up the fight. Morris staggered across the creek and collapsed on the opposite bank. Until then, it was unclear how bad he was hurt. He was taken to the hospital in Century, FL. The knife wounds were very close to his heart, but the doctor felt he would survive. He was concerned, however, that infection would set in due to Morris going into the water after he was stabbed. Sure enough, infection set in, and then pneumonia resulting in his death on 3 March.

Ed Morris was buried at the Halls Creek Church cemetery. The Red Sox sent outfielder, and friend Tommy Oliver to the funeral to represent the team. Big Ed's mother Ella died in 1940, and she was buried next to him.

Thirty-Six-year-old Joe White was arrested, tried, and found guilty of manslaughter. He was sentenced to three years, but the conviction was reversed by the Alabama Court of Appeals. There was a retrial in August 1934, in Brewton Alabama, and White was found not guilty.

Ed's Family
Ed married Beryl Tompkins of Bullock Co., Alabama in 1924. She was born on 10 March 1905, and died 5 June 1985. She is buried at the Pine Crest Cemetery, in Mobile, Alabama.

He had two sons:

    Edward Morris, b. 29 Jun 1925, d. 2 Feb 1991, also buried at the Pine Crest Cemetery.
    Mortimer T. Morris, b. 10 July 1927, d. 30 Mar 2000. He is buried at Serenity Memorial Gardens in Theodore, Mobile Co., Alabama.

    Interesting post script about Ed's wife Beryl. She got remarried a few months after Ed's death to Dr. Joseph E. Rose, who was 25 years older than her and had recently divorced his wife, Ida, who he had been married to since 1909. There is a marriage record of a wedding in Desha County, Arkansas on 30 Nov 1932, and a second record in Walton Co., Florida on 15 Dec 1932. Beryl divorced her second husband in Bradford Co., Florida in 1950. He then remarried his first wife Ida. He died in 1958, and is buried at Bayview cemetery in Pensacola.

The Ed Morris Baseball Progression

1920- Bradenton- Florida State League

1921- Chattanooga- Class A- Southern Association. Record of 9-21 with 4.48 ERA.

1922- Chattanooga- 5-19, 4.85 ERA.

1922- briefly called up to the Chicago Cubs. Pitched 12 innings in relief with an ERA of 8.25.

1923- Chattanooga, and the Nashville Volunteers. 9-11 with 5.58 ERA.

1925- Spring- Tryout with Cincinnati Reds. Sore arm and sent back to Nashville.
At Nashville he was 17-11 with 4.52 ERA.
1926- Nashville- 16-13 4.53 ERA.

1927-Mobile Bay Bears- Southern Association- 298 innings pitched. 15-17 3.96 ERA.

1928- Boston Red Sox- May 3, first victory against the Phil. Athletics. 4-hitter. Through August 25th, his record was 17-11, with a 3.13 ERA. He went downhill from there, and finished the season 19-15 with a 3.53 era, and 257 innings pitched. Still good enough to be the best rookie pitcher in the league, for the worst team in the league.

1929- Suffered arm Problems. Finished 14-14 with a 4.45 era. 208 IP, 73K, 95BB.

1930- Salary holdout. Red Sox spring training in Pensacola. Finally signed for $500 raise to $8,000. More arm problems and he finished with a 4-9 record,4.13 ERA.

1931- Pensacola spring training again. Season record 5-7, 4.75 era. Though he improved toward the end of the season, and was anticipating a better performance in 1932, his dismal record was the result of "injuries, and failure to condition." His last pitching performance was a complete game 4-hit 9-2 victory over the St. Louis Browns. It was his last appearance.

> Official report of Morris' death as issued from Turberville hospital yesterday was as follows: "Morris died of a massive collapse of lungs and general pleuritis of the left side due to knife wounds, of chest walls, one of which was punctured."

Pensacola Journal 4 March 1932

Four Years of Ed's Salary

        1928 $3500.   In 2019 dollars- $51,706
        1929 $7500   "   "   "   " $110,799
        1930 $8000 $121,482
        1931 $4000 $66,722

Chapter Eleven

Killer on the Road

Apparently, on a whim, and desiring to get his hands on some quick cash, Harvey McGraw, 20, decided to rob Jaxon's Filling Station, just south of Georgiana, Alabama. On the evening of March 16, 1939, he killed some time loitering at the station, claiming he was waiting on a bus, as Jaxon's was also a Greyhound bus station. As the hour neared midnight at the all-night station, two men from the Montgomery area arrived at the station. One report states that the two men, Clifford T. Mann, 28, and Charles Wilkinson, 23, were in the station drinking a glass of milk, and they intended on renting one of the available cabins for the night. McGraw asked the attendant, Dennis Moore, for change for a quarter. When Moore opened the register, McGraw produced a weapon and demanded the money. Different descriptions of the robbery say it was either $24, or $37. He then forced the two men into their car at gunpoint. Getting into the back seat, he told Mann to head south.

McGraw had the misfortune of choosing a target for his robbery that was equipped with a Police Transmission Radio Set. The State Patrol had strategically placed these in locations around the state. Dennis Moore immediately transmitted a call alerting Patrolmen Thigpen, and Sawyer in Georgiana of the robbery, and kidnapping. Calls went out to Mobile, and Pensacola, and a net was spread through southern Alabama.

McGraw was smart enough to keep away from the larger towns. He later was heard to say that he made Mann drive at speeds of 70 to 90 miles per hour. From the Greenville Advocate, March 30, 1939, "He had them leave U.S. 31 at McKensie, 6 miles south of the robbery site. At Red Level he left the McKensie-Andalusia highway and took a short cut over to the Andalusia-Brewton highway. At East Brewton he switched to the Brewton-Milton highway." By taking this route he was able to avoid officers watching the towns of Evergreen, Andalusia, and Brewton. The car ran out of gas about 8 miles north of Milton, near the Allentown community.

He made Mann, and Wilkinson get out of the car and began to tie them together, when according to McGraw when telling the story later, one of the men made a grab at the pistol. He shot him, and then shot the other one for trying to intervene in the struggle. It should be noted that both men were shot several times in the head, chest, and the back.

About a half of a mile away, farmer Turpen Wiggins, (the newspaper articles use Williams, but no Turpen Williams can be found), heard what he thought was a series of automobile backfires around 3:30 am. Later around 8:30 he saw a vehicle parked about 200 yards off the road and walked over to investigate, where he found the two bodies tied together.

Who Was Harvey McGraw?

Harvey was the son of Elmer McGraw, a well-known resident of the Appleton community which lies north of Brewton. He was on parole from the Atmore prison after serving 6 months of a 1-to-5-year sentence for attempted burglary. He twice in one night tried to enter the home of W.F. Dantzler on the Appleton Road, but was frightened away both times. He was convicted in October 1937. Harvey was known in the Brewton area, and had once worked in the Box Factory of the T.R. Miller Company.

The Victims

Clifford T. Mann was originally from Elmore County, Alabama, but moved to Montgomery to engage in the Real Estate business. About four years before his murder, he became associated with the Praetorian Life Insurance company. He later became the General Agent, and office manager for the district.

Charles Wilkinson was a native of Montgomery, and currently unemployed. Previously he was a traveling salesman. He was accompanying his friend on his business trip at the time of the abduction.

The Capture

A cab driver named Dick Carpenter, had a radio in his taxi. He heard a broadcast of the wanted murderer/kidnapper, and thought of a fare he had earlier driven from Milton to the L&N depot in Pensacola. He remembered the fare because the guy said he was going to catch a train heading east, which would have passed back through Milton. Carpenter alerted the police who contacted Sheriff Harrell in Chipley, Florida.

Sheriff Harrell boarded the train when it reached Chipley with a description of the wanted man. He approached McGraw and took him into custody. McGraw did make an attempt to use his pistol, but the Sheriff disarmed him and removed him from the train.

After the Arrest

McGraw immediately confessed to the kidnapping, and killing of Mann, and Wilkinson. Alabama could have tried him for armed robbery, which at the time, could have resulted in the death penalty. The Federal Government, also, could have tried him for kidnapping under the Lindbergh Law which could have resulted in a death sentence. Both Alabama, and the Feds were content to let Florida handle the trial, and punishment.

He quickly became known as a happy-go-lucky young man who liked to sing and play guitar. He had an abundance of talent and people would visit to listen to him perform. On May 3, a routine cell inspection found a pistol, fashioned from a bar of soap, was discovered. There was one humorous report that he tried to break out of jail and when he brandished his soap gun at a guard, the barrel fell off, exposing his ruse. Sheriff Joe Allen denied that that had happened. He said it was found in the search.

At the end of May an arraignment was held with Circuit Judge L.L. Fabisinski and McGraw pled guilty to two counts of first-degree murder, throwing himself on the mercy of the court. The proceeding had to be delayed for a few hours because McGraw was under 21 so his father, Elmer, had to be retrieved from the Castleberry, Alabama area to attend the arraignment. His court-appointed attorney, Woodrow Melvin had a conference with the McGraw's to give them options, but Harvey insisted on the guilty pleas. He was heard to say, "What's the use? I'm going to burn anyway". The following day Judge Fabisinski sentenced McGraw to death.

Either, just before, or just after his court appearances, Harvey McGraw was baptized in Pond Creek on Highway 90, west of Milton. His grandfather, Sherman McGraw was a Holiness Minister, and had visited Harvey in jail. When the Judge was asked if he could be baptized, he said it was up to Sheriff Allen. The Sheriff, at least two deputies, and about 30 Holiness preachers led by E.G. Holley, met a Pond Creek. Harvey wearing a white shirt, and dungarees, and handcuffed to Deputy Purvis Baxley, Sr., (whose son Purvis, Jr. years later was the first principal of King Middle School), stepped into the water and was baptized. "I feel saved now", was all he had to say.

On June 17 it was reported in the Pensacola Journal that Harvey gave a statement through his attorney, Woodrow Melvin, for publication in the area's newspapers.

"I wish to express my extreme regrets for the crimes I have committed, trusting that the public will realize that I KNOW what a terrible deed it was. I trust that folks who think that the only reason I am grateful is because I was caught and sentenced, will change their views on the matter. Everyone knows that I entered pleas of guilty at my trial in circuit court here last month, which proved that I wasn't seeking to evade justice."

Harvey McGraw

On September 4, 1939, approximately 6 months since he committed the crimes, Harvey McGraw was led to the execution chamber at Raiford prison. At 10:06 am, Sheriff Joe T. Allen "turned the rheostat" which sent the current through his body. McGraw made no final statement to the 38 witnesses but he did silently mouth the Lord's Prayer while it was recited by Prison Chaplain, Rev. Leslie Sheppard.

McGraw's father and uncle were at the prison but did not go to the death chamber. They were there to take his body back home for burial. The paper claimed he was going to be buried at the Center Grove cemetery, north of Brewton. Actually, his remains, along with other family members are located at the Zion Hill Baptist Church cemetery.

Clifford T. Mann left a widow. He married Eva Louise Glover in Montgomery on April 18, 1936. She also worked for the same Insurance Company, and they had no children.

Charles Wilkinson also left a widow, but no children. He married Mary Lou Hughes on Jun 21, 1938 in Montgomery.

The two friends who were just in the wrong place, at the wrong time are both buried in Section One at the Greenwood Cemetery in Montgomery.

Jaxon's Service Station was a well-known establishment in southern Alabama. It was located on Highway 31, about one mile south of Georgiana. It was also a Greyhound Bus station, and had tourist cabins to rent by travelers.

Picture from The Milton Gazette

Chapter Twelve

The Burden of Guilt

The Crime

At 2 am on 1951's Easter Sunday, a truck driver from Chickasaw, Alabama named J.W. Kitchens, stopped to refuel at Joe Guidry's Standard Oil Service station, at the intersection of Hwy 98, and State Road 85, near the Indian Mound in downtown Ft. Walton Beach. Upon entering the station, he found the body of the attendant, Romeo A. Beaudry, a crippled ex-pilot who was working there on his scheduled night off.

Kitchens spread the alarm, and soon was joined by night-policeman Buck Burnham, and Constable Oscar Bengtson. The victim had been shot 4 times, twice near the heart, once in the throat, and once above the left eye. There was no evidence of a robbery. The next morning Paul, and Arthur Bond, children of the Spanish Villa operator, discovered a .32 caliber pistol hidden beneath a piece of tin, on the Indian mound, and turned it over to the police.

The Victim

Romeo Albert Beaudry was almost 50 years old the night he died. He lived in the Santa Rosa Community about 15 miles east of Ft. Walton Beach. His background is not well documented. He was born in Baltimore, Maryland 30 March 1901. He was in the U.S. Army as a Private in the 38th Infantry from Nov. 1923 to April 1927. His WW2 draft registration shows him living in Washington Co, Mississippi in Feb. 1942. He had worked for a time at Nowak Radio and Appliance Service in Warrington, Escambia Co., Florida off and on for a few years, and had left there in mid-February, shortly before beginning his job at the

Standard Oil Station at the highway 90 intersection in downtown Ft. Walton Beach.

On early Easter morning when he was killed, he was wearing a red jockey hat with Army Air Corp wings. It is unclear when he would have earned them unless it was during his time in the Mississippi National Guard. In WW2 he was in Norfolk, Virginia as a radioman working in a shipyard. A couple of nights before he was killed, he talked to a local reporter, Jane McCreary, of the Playground News. He told her he had been injured in a crash during his service. "There's hardly a part of me that hasn't been patched up". Injuries kept him in hospitals for years, and got him a disability pension from the government. He told the reporter that he had lived in Jackson, Miss., where he met and married his wife and operated a radio shop. He was a member of the Mississippi National Guard, and had piloted a crop duster, spraying cotton fields for the boll weevil. He was an honorary game warden and an insomniac who sometimes wandered the streets at night. He spoke fluent French, and also drove an ambulance for the McLaughlin Funeral Home in Ft. Walton Beach. He told the reporter, "Civilization is nothing but refined barbarism".

The Investigation

There were no obvious clues left at the scene. Beaudry wore braces on his legs that had to be adjusted before he could stand. Since there seemed to be no attempt to stand, and a partially eaten sandwich on the desk, it was then assumed that the murder was committed by someone known to the victim. The gun found by the Bond children was traced to a shop in Pensacola. It had been purchased on 13 February, but there was no record of the buyer. Beaudry had started working at the station around that same time, and Constable Bengtson learned that Beaudry's wife Cora, had taken out an insurance policy on the 2nd of February. By April 1, a reward of $1200 had not been claimed, and "all leads were exhausted". Then in walks 19-year-old William Whoolery.

On July 31, 1951, Constable Bengtson announced the arrests of William Dickson Connerly, a Pensacola radio repairman on a murder charge. Also arrested was the victim's wife Cora Beaudry as an accessory. Also held was a 19-year-old Destin fisherman named William Homer Woolery.

    Constable Bengtson said that on Sunday, July 29, William Whoolery came into his office and claimed that he knew who killed Beaudry, because the victim's widow had told him. Bengtson then began using Whoolery as an undercover investigator because he lived near the Beaudry home. The 19-year-old claimed that Mrs. Beaudry had tried to kill herself, by taking pills, and while being driven to the White Clinic in Ft. Walton Beach, tried to jump out of the moving vehicle. Dr. White, at the clinic later told Bengtson that he thought Mrs. Beaudry had swallowed about 20 aspirin tablets, and about 8 phenobarbital pills. He said when she was brought into his clinic she was in a, "highly nervous, and excited condition." When asked if he could tell if she had ingested phenobarbital, the Doctor said, "I don't think it was anything else."

    Whoolery claimed that while at the clinic, Mrs. Beaudry told his parents to "Go get Willie", because she wanted to tell him who did it. Bond was set at $5000 for Connerly, and $2500 for Mrs. Beaudry. Whoolery requested to remain in jail for the time being. From his cell, Connerly, a Pensacola Naval Air Station Radio Mechanic, and former vocational school instructor said, "It was the greatest shock of my life when 'Lou' Beaudry was killed", then a greater shock when he was arrested. "I'm charged with the murder of my best friend." Connerly said he and Beaudry met in Jackson, Mississippi in February of 1942 when both were members of the state guard. When the two families moved to the Panhandle, they remained in touch. "I can prove I was attending a wake, and a funeral the night Lou was killed".

    In her cell, Mrs. Beaudry said she did not believe Connerly killed her husband. She also denied attempting suicide. "I've got two children; I'm not going to do anything that will bring shame to them". She said she asked the Whoolery's to take her to the hospital when she had a gallbladder attack, and had taken 4 to 5 aspirin. She also said she had discussed her husband's death with Whoolery, and had mentioned Connerly, but had never accused him of the murder.

On the 3rd of August, the Pensacola Journal reported that Connerly had been released from jail on a writ of habeas corpus filed by his Pensacola attorney, Richard Merritt. The finding was that there was insufficient evidence. In the same hearing, Mrs. Beaudry was to remain in jail due to testimony from Whoolery, and his mother, who both said they had heard her say she knew who did it. The charges against Connerly were dropped.

Mrs. Cora Beaudry was released 30 August when an Okaloosa Grand Jury refused to indict her. She eventually remarried and passed away in 2001 while living on the Kenai Peninsula in Alaska.

There was another man detained by Constable Bengtson named William Floyd Carnley. He was questioned for a few hours, and released. This was done without a warrant. Of course, his name was later listed in the local newspapers as a suspect in the killing. In 1952, two $50,000 lawsuits for malicious prosecution, and false arrest were brought against Bengtson by both Connerly, and Carnley. Both suits were thrown out in July.

Mr. X confesses to a Cold Case

On March 7, 1963, a married construction worker with three children living in Johnstown, NY confessed to his priest about killing a crippled man during a botched service station robbery in Ft. Walton Beach, Florida early on Easter morning back in 1951. Easter was approaching and the christening of his 8-month-old child was to be held Sunday. The priest talked him into going to a local attorney, Mario Albanese. The attorney called Ft. Walton Police Chief Ralph Hendrix and said a client had told him he knew something about the Beaudry case. His confession was due to a heavy burden of guilt with the possibility that some innocent person had been punished for the crime.

Reporters from the Pensacola Journal learned of the confession and the man's name, and location. They called Attorney Albanese, and he confirmed the name of his client. The reporter then called his client and he was more than willing to tell the Journal his story. He claimed he and a companion were involved in the killing, and he had let the authorities know the name of his accomplice. He also said that he could not remember exactly if he had pulled the trigger. He claimed they had been drinking at The Spanish Villa shortly before they decided to rob the gas station.

The Journal referred to the man as "Mr. X", because he hadn't been arrested, or charged at the time they talked to him. Mr. X revealed that at the time of the murder, he, and his companion were Air Policemen at Eglin, AFB in Ft. Walton. After the killing, they went AWOL and were both arrested for robbery in Maryland. He served one year of a three-year sentence and stayed out of trouble, getting married and having three children before his confession.

In the Saturday issue of the Pensacola Journal, Mr. X was revealed to be Anthony F. Glionna, of Johnstown, New York. He was being detained in New York. Sheriff Ray Wilson, and State Attorney William Frye were in Baltimore to arrest Glionna's alleged accomplice.

There were extradition hearings in both New York, and Baltimore for the two suspects, and on April 5, 1963, it was reported that Deputy Reubin Hendrix departed for Johnstown, NY to return Glionna to Crestview for trial. A hearing to return Glionna's alleged accomplice, Walter Richard Allen, was scheduled, but Allen waived extradition and was transported to Okaloosa County. Glionna's extradition papers were signed by New York Governor Rockefeller and he was turned over to Okaloosa Deputy Driscoll Oglesby on April 5. They both arrived at the Okaloosa County Jail within hours of each other. On 10 April they were both arraigned and entered pleas of innocence.

On May 3, an Okaloosa Grand Jury returned a true bill indicting Anthony Glionna with First Degree murder in the death of Romeo Beaudry. Since April 29, Glionna had been at the State Mental Hospital in Chattahoochee when court-appointed psychiatrists found that he was not capable of assisting with his defense. Walter Richard Allen had been granted immunity by State Attorney Bill Frye, and was to be used as a prosecution witness.

Walter Richard Allen's Story:

Allen sat for a two-hour interview after his testimony at the Grand Jury proceedings. This is from the Pensacola New-Journal, Sunday, May 5, 1963.

"Glionna and I were both stationed in the Air Police Squadron at Eglin Field. We were the best of friends, where one went the other went. We just seemed to be compatible, and in fact, he was the only person with whom I had ever been close until that point in my life.

"Glionna was a three-striper at the time and I was a one-striper. I had been at the base for about a year and Glionna had been there for two years. On the night of the slaying, we did not go into town together, although I'm not now sure of the reason. It could have been one of us had a date, or one had late duty or some other reason. We first met that night in town, and this is not hard to do in Fort Walton Beach in 1951 because the entire community was centered in just four blocks along Main Street.

"At first sight it was apparent that Tony was different than I had seen him before, because he showed me a pistol and said he intended to do away with the town constable, (The late Oscar Bengtson), with whom he had been involved in an altercation much earlier. He was heading toward the constable's office on Main Street and I talked long and hard and pulled at him to keep away from completing his mission. We walked on past after a delay in front of the office and continued the argument about doing away with the constable and then we entered the Hi Hat where we ordered a drink.

"Tony produced the gun below the level of the bar and threatened to kill the owner and his wife and I quickly pushed him toward the door. I didn't feel that I was in danger myself because throughout the arguments he acted as though he needed me. We started the argument again about his intention of killing someone and after we passed the Spanish Villa, I finally left him and returned either to the bar or café portion of the Spanish Villa. I was tired of arguing and told him he was on his own.

"It was only a short time later, maybe 10, or at most 15 minutes, when he came in and said he had shot the service station attendant and threw the gun away. He told me that I was in it with him and asked what we should do. The only thing I could think was to get back to the base. We hailed a taxi and made the trip to the base in complete silence and that was the last time that we ever talked of the murder until we met again in the Crestview jail. It seemed to build a barrier between us, and at the same time it caused a kinship to develop that I couldn't seem to shake.

"We both remained at Eglin for a period of five months and contrary to some reports, I did not go AWOL, (Absent, without Leave), from Eglin. I worked for a transfer and finally got shipping orders to the west coast and Tony decided that we should not be separated and he decided to go AWOL and returned to Baltimore with me on my delayed leave. We ran out of money on the way and decided to hold up a grocery store, along with another boy that had joined us. We pulled the job and got caught and after being sentenced and while in jail I was declared AWOL.

"After we finished our time on that sentence and were paroled, I remained in Baltimore and Tony went back to his home in New York. I saw him only one time before being returned to Crestview and that was about a year after we were released from the Maryland reformatory. He came to Baltimore and suggested that I should join him on a trip to Miami. We spent several weeks in Miami and in New Orleans and at the result of breaking our parole. I felt that someday Tony would tell about it but all those years I just kept trying to disappear.

"When I learned of Glionna's statement implicating me, I felt he had done it to prove a reason for the slaying, but after talking with friends in Baltimore I decided to turn myself in and face the consequences, although with my record I felt it was five-to-one against me. After I stood in the Baltimore Police Station for a few minutes, I walked on out another door without talking to anyone. Then I decided to return and went straight to a telephone and called my friend before *asking for Sgt. Callahan of the fugitive squad. Callahan had been the officer that visited my friends and I'll have to admit that he played fair with me and kept me posted on the case. In fact, it was his information about Glionna being extradited that led me to agree to waive extradition and head for Okaloosa County to have the thing over with.*

"I saw Tony soon after I arrived in Crestview, and although we exchanged greetings and shook hands in the lobby of the jail we didn't really talk. It was one of those things like, 'Hi, Al, how are you?' 'I'm fine and you, Tony?' Even after they moved Tony into a cell by himself, a cell next to the one in which I was being held we still didn't really talk except for Tony asking for cigarettes.

"It's hard to explain what I felt I would find when I was brought back here, but it was pretty rough territory when I left and there didn't seem to be much possibility that it had changed. Since we've been in Crestview, I've spotted several people that I'd known while stationed at Eglin. It seems that a great many of them are either still here or have retired or settled in the Eglin area."

Allen became a trustee during his time in the Okaloosa County jail after being granted immunity by Judge Charles A. Wade on a petition filed by State Attorney William Frye. The state wanted to use him in Glionna's prosecution.

Allen soon was released with the promise to return when, and if, Glionna stood trial. In the Sacramento Bee on Feb 15, 1964, there is a report of Walter Richard Allen charged with the burglary of the West Sacramento Post Office on November 27. Charged with theft of government property, and bail was set at $5000. I haven't been able so far to find any further information about Allen.

Glionna

Over the next few years Anthony Glionna was returned to Okaloosa County periodically for examination to determine if he was mentally able to stand trial for the Beaudry murder. In 1966 during one of his examination periods, Glionna went on a hunger strike in the Okaloosa County jail. Sheriff Wilson returned him to Chattahoochee.

In February 1974, the murder charges were dropped. Glionna had been committed to the State Mental Hospital in Chattahoochee since 1963 when it was determined that he exhibited Schizophrenic, and psychotic behavior. While dropping the charges Assistant State Attorney Walter Anderson notified the court that the chain of evidence was "hopelessly broken". He cited the deaths of material witnesses, including some investigators, and the fact that Glionna did not have counsel before he confessed and the possibility that he may have been insane at the time. Anthony lived until 26 March 1998 when he passed away in Camillus, Onondaga County, New York.

An interesting sidebar to this case is the State Attorney William Frye. When the original crime was committed in 1951, he was a member of the same Air Police unit that Glionna, and Allen were members of. In 1963 he was the State Attorney who traveled to New York to investigate the claims of guilt made by Glionna, and would have prosecuted him if he went to trial. In 1972, Frye was the District Circuit Judge where Glionna was released.

Before Bullet Cut Him Down

Romeo A. Beaudry is shown here shortly before he was found shot to death in a Fort Walton Beach gasoline station Easter morning, 1951. Beaudry's bullet-riddled body was found at 2 a.m. slumped backward in a chair in the station he attended at U.S. 98-State Road 85 Intersection. He had been shot at close range and no money had been taken from the cash register. Beaudry was 49 at the time.

Pensacola Journal 8 March 1963

Chapter Thirteen

The Hanging of Wayman King

(From, The Daily News, Pensacola, Florida, March 9, 1900)

WAYMAN KING HANGED TWICE

Murderer of Victoria Watkins Pays the Penalty

Drop Fell at 1:05 Sharp

But After the Body Was Cut Down, It Was Found That He Was Still Alive

He Was Hanged Again At 1:29

King was perfectly calm and smiling. Called for and shook hands with a number of People he knew– Father McCafferty and Father English Administer Last Rites of Catholic Church.

Wayman King was hanged in jail yard this afternoon.

At 12:10 o'clock the condemned man was brought from the cell and escorted to the gallows by Sheriff Smith, Deputies Frank Sanders, Hal Cowart, and Aaron Kelly, and accompanied by Father McCafferty and Father English of St. Michael's Catholic Church. Chaplain H. W. Jones of the Navy yard and five colored ministers walked up the fourteen steps to the elevated gallows.

Originally there were thirteen steps leading up to the gallows, but at the request of King, an additional step was added.

Having ascended to the platform Wayman King, dressed in a neat new black suit, looked around at the assembled multitude in the jail yard, in the streets, on buildings for blocks away and with calm indifference said he would like to shake hands with people he saw around that he knew.

At his request, Ed Goldstuker, James Farinas, Frank Benjamin, Fred Humphreys, Andrew Bolline, Dr. F. G. Renshaw, C. B. Parkhill, Dr. D. W. McMillan, A. M. McMillan in turn came up and shook hands with the condemned man. At 12:20 a colored minister ascended the steps and he and Wayman King knelt while the minister prayed fervently that the soul of King might be saved.

Hans Kelly and Ed Amos then went up at the request of King and shook hands with him.

Sheriff Mitchell of Santa Rosa County, who captured King, was near the gallows and King saw him and called him up to bid him goodbye.

At 12:28, in a low calm voice, he addressed the great throng of people, saying:

"White and colored Gentlemen: I am sorry to be in such a terrible condition, but am glad to know that I have made peace with God. I have lots to say but my time is too short. I am surprised to see so many colored people laughing and pointing at me while I am in this terrible condition. Every one of them will have their day to answer for this. I did not get justice in my trial. I think it a most horrible thing that I should be hanged when Reuben Harris who killed Officer Yelverten was let off with life sentence in the penitentiary. There was no justice in that.

"As for Sheriff Smith, I think him the best man for the office. He has been very kind to me and has given me everything that was in his power to give."

His voice then became so low the reporter could not catch the close of his address.

Engineer Caro, a member of the jury who convicted him. C. Moreno Jones, Marshal Frank Wilde, Nico Giardiana, John Thompson, Conductor Geo. White, Julius Menko and C. P. Bobe were then in turn called and shook hands with King.

The doomed man then calmly lit and smoked a cigar, and as he shook hands with Engineer Sizer looking around and smiling at the crowd.

He then called for a chew of tobacco. Aaron Kelly handed him a piece but he did not like the brand and gave it back. Several pieces were tossed up to him and he finally found a piece to suit him and chewed it vigorously.

At 12:52 Father McCafferty read to him from the Bible. At 12:58 Father McCafferty held the Holy Crucifix to King's face and administered the Last Rites of the Catholic church. He then shook hands with the holy father, stepped upon the trap, his hands and feet were securely bound by Deputy Sheriff Aaron Kelly. The noose was fitted around his neck, the black cap was put on and at 1:05 pm the trap was pulled and Wayman King went down to death.

City Physician D. W. McMillan put his hand upon the pulse and felt the life flutter away. At 1:10 pm he pronounced him dead and he was cut down, put in a coffin and carried into the jail.

There it was found that King was not dead, but was breathing in jerks and uttering smothered groans.

By order of the Sheriff, King was taken back to the gallows, a new rope was rigged, the noose was readjusted and at 1:29 pm the trap was pulled the second time. At 1:40 Dr. McMillan declared him dead and, after hanging four minutes longer, he was cut down at 1:49 pm. The body will be buried at 5 o'clock this afternoon.

There was an immense throng of people in town to see the execution and they were massed in solid array in the streets around the jail and were hanging on thick from the tops of buildings for several blocks around– wherever a view of the jail yard could be had.

When the drop fell several women in the crowd fainted and others shouted, sang hymns and raved in an excited manner.

History of the Crime

The crime for which Wayman King was legally executed today was the murder of Victoria Watkins on September 16th, at a house near St. John's cemetery.

It seems that King and the Watkins woman had been keeping company for some time and she frequently urged him to arrange for marriage, but he put her off from time to time.

Finally, on Friday, Sept. 15, having grown tired of his procrastination, the Watkins woman jilted King and told him that she would not talk about marriage with him again until he displayed some interest in getting ready for the event. King begged her to reconsider her verdict, but she was obdurate and King finally told her that he was going to leave town that night, but would make her sorry she had refused him before he did leave.

King did not leave town that night but returned to the house several times Saturday morning, Sept. 16, to again press his suit, but the Watkins woman turned a deaf ear to his pleas.

That afternoon he returned to the house again and it is alleged that while the woman was sweeping in one of the rooms he shot at her through the open window, using a 44-caliber pistol. The ball entered the left side and penetrated the woman's bowels. She was carried to the Infirmary for treatment and died there at 10 o'clock that night. King escaped, but was captured near Milton, Sunday, Sept. 17, by Sheriff

Mitchell of Santa Rosa County and was brought here that night and lodged in jail.

In the circuit court on December 7, 1899, Judge J. R. Wall, presiding. Wayman King was found guilty of murder in the first degree. He was later sentenced to be hanged, and today he paid the penalty of his crime.

The Reuben Harris that King referred to in his final statement was found guilty of killing Police Officer J. G. Yelverton. Initially Harris was sentenced to hang, but his sentence was commuted to a life term later.

I guess there is really no tradition about setting someone free if they survive the first execution attempt.

This was transcribed from the original article.

Milton Keynes UK
Ingram Content Group UK Ltd.
UKHW020622100823
426637UK00013B/464